# Science and ICT
## • in the •
# Primary
# School

the information store

CHALLENGING MINDS. INSPIRING SUCCESS.

CITY COLLEGE
NORWICH

# Science and ICT
## • in the •
# Primary School

## A Creative Approach to Big Ideas

## John Meadows

**David Fulton** Publishers

This edition reprinted 2007 by Routledge
2 Park Square, Milton Park, Abingdon, Oxon, OX14 4RN
Simultaneously published in the USA and Canada
By Routledge
270 Madison Avenue, New York, NY 10016

First published in Great Britain in 2004 by David Fulton Publishers
Reprinted 2005

10 9 8 7 6 5 4 3

Note: The right of John Meadows to be identified as the author of this work has been
asserted by him in accordance with the Copyright, Designs and Patents Act 1988.

*British Library Cataloguing in Publication Data*
A catalogue record for this book is available from the British Library.

ISBN: 1 84312 120 4

Typeset by RefineCatch Limited, Bungay, Suffolk
Printed and bound in Great Britain

# Contents

# Acknowledgements

Thanks to the student teachers who allowed me to watch, take notes and discuss their work. These included Katie, Heidi, Richard, Luciana and Louise, as well as Natalee, Lyndsey, Fiona and Claire.

Thanks also to the primary schools, many which I have visited and gained a lot of ideas from, especially Hargrave Park, Montem, Hollickwood, St John's, St John and St James, Burbage, Chalgrove and Stamford Hill.

Finally, thanks to colleagues at work, who helped me to complete this in lots of ways, especially Chris Horner, whose critical comments helped me to straighten out some of my more tortuous sentences, and Sally, Jean and Peter, whose support was invaluable.

# Preface

This book is written mainly for student teachers and newly qualified teachers; it provides a rationale for the emphasis on teaching and learning of big ideas as well as suggesting that a creative approach to teaching is important. The whole book has a special focus on helping teachers to think for themselves and on them helping the children to think, within a framework of statutory requirements like outcomes, clear learning objectives, clear assessment techniques and recording routines.

The first chapter explains what is meant by a creative approach to teaching and explores the notion that there are big ideas in the content and processes of science. It then looks at ways of teaching with ICT and at children learning with ICT.

Chapter 2 introduces some of the major theories of teaching and learning, and shows how they have been used to justify approaches to the teaching of science and ICT in primary schools.

Chapter 3 presents several case studies of student teachers working in primary schools, describing the settings and environments and the ways in which these students managed to use ICT in their teaching of science.

The focus in Chapter 4 is on the big idea of flight and this chapter examines ways of teaching, starting with feathers and birds, then looking at objects that spin as they fall through the air and finally at making and testing parachutes, while using databases and spreadsheets to record and present the results.

In Chapter 5, the big idea is sustainability in teacher training and in schools. The chapter shows how younger children can be introduced to the complexities of investigating ourselves, other animals and environments.

Chapter 6 deals with light, colour, shadows and vision. It also shows how to use digital cameras and light meters in support of the objectives of science teaching.

Chapter 7 begins with the idea that there are opportunities in our everyday lives and in the lives and experiences of children that can lead to useful and relevant teaching and learning in science and ICT. Contexts such as the kitchen are used as examples of the links between school learning and learning in everyday life.

Energy is the big idea in Chapter 8 and it is exemplified through a look at energy transformations, forces and movement, energy and food, and the concept of being alive.

Materials and the existence of particles is the big idea that underpins Chapter 9. This chapter starts with the question: 'What if a chair was made of chocolate?' It goes on to suggest the exploration of a variety of materials including water as liquid and solid.

The big idea in Chapter 10 is the existence of cells. The way that living things are organised on a microscopic level into cells of various types is approached at a macroscopic level through activities and observations on living things, including plants, ourselves, our senses, the human digestive system, and the functions of heart and blood.

Chapter 11 presents several scenarios for dealing with learning out of school. We have already looked at learning from everyday life in Chapter 7; Chapter 11 suggests ideas for visiting public places like museums, or using buildings as a starting point, studying in the built and in the natural environment.

Finally, in Chapter 12, we look at managing the learning, and organising children and resources in the classroom, further ideas about planning lessons and sequences of lessons, crossing the curriculum and assessing children's progress.

Most chapters have a common format, with an introduction, learning outcomes, tables showing ICT National Curriculum links and links to science and ICT QCA schemes. Each chapter is split into three or four sections, dealing with both science and ICT teaching and learning, and there is a short summary at the end of each.

In some chapters there are Directed Activities, that can be used to help to focus attention on specific teaching or resource ideas. In some, there are resources that can be used with pupils, to support their recording of activities. Throughout the book, there is an emphasis on the importance of linking theory with practice. The emphasis on creativity means that there is limited prescription in the instructions given and that alternative approaches are suggested for teachers and children.

There is a short glossary dealing with some of the meanings of scientific words, as well as the inevitable acronyms that appear in any book dealing with education. Words that appear in the glossary are indicated in the text in bold type with quote marks around them, like '**energy**'. Each chapter has a web links section at the end, and all the references are shown at the end of the book.

# What's it all about?
# A creative approach to big ideas

## Introduction

This chapter defines a view of what big ideas about science and information and communications technology (ICT) might be and why they are important in primary school teaching. It is supported, in the second chapter of the book, by educational theory stretching over many years as well as by current thinking about what constitutes good primary school teaching and learning. This chapter deals with two main issues: firstly, what does a creative approach to teaching mean and then, what are big ideas? Section 1.1 explores what a creative approach could mean; sections 1.2 and 1.3 deal with science; while sections 1.4 and 1.5 focus more on ICT.

## What is a creative approach?

A creative approach to teaching and learning demands a certain expectation of the reader of this book – you should not be hoping to get lesson plans from it that you can just use straight away in your own classrooms. There are plenty of other places where these are available; see websites (http://www.educate.org.uk/) and books like Letts guides (Peacock 1999). This book does not attempt to explain lots of science knowledge or concepts – again, there are other places where this can be found. What this book does do is suggest ways to put theory, knowledge, skills and creativity into practice. A creative approach means taking some of the ideas presented here and adapting them, using your own ideas, so that they can be used to support teaching and learning in your own classroom.

## What are big ideas?

In science they can be about content, like:

'**Cells**' exist, and can be seen with a microscope.

'**Particles**' are thought to exist even if we cannot see them.

'**Gravity**' is a force that attracts objects towards each other.

'**Light**' is needed to help us to see.

Or big ideas could be about teaching science, such as:

It is necessary to make the imperceptible perceptible.

Children's ideas are important starting points for teaching.

Teachers should help children to move from the particular to the general.

Children should be encouraged to predict before testing.

In ICT the big ideas are different, partly because ICT depends more on skills and techniques than on concepts (although there are models and ideas too), so the big ideas are presented as major reasons for using ICT in science teaching.

ICT is used in primary schools in two main ways:

- as a tool to help teachers deliver the curriculum;
- to help children learn better.

## ICT is not the same as IT

The 'C' in ICT means communication and implies the process of communication and the reasons for its importance, rather than just the technological background to it and how it works. This book does not try to cover the teaching of information technology skills, or how to use computers and digital devices themselves. It does try to focus on how children can be helped to learn through the use of information and communications technology, rather than how to learn IT, and it also suggests how teachers can use ICT to support their teaching. Hence the focus on big ideas in ICT is intended to suggest ways, for example that word processing can help in learning and teaching science, or how databases can help children understand patterns in science.

## Reasons for using ICT in teaching science

It is possible to identify a number of reasons for using ICT. Have a look at the following sets of justifications and compare them to your own views. Here are five realistic reasons for using ICT in science teaching in primary schools:

1  It is statutory in the England and Wales National Curriculum to teach both science and ICT in primary schools.

2  During initial teacher training and the induction period in the first year of teaching, it is also statutory for trainees to use ICT and to teach science – this is governed by QTT standards 2.5 and others.

3  Using ICT makes science teaching more fun – it allows both children and their teachers to enjoy teaching and learning more because ICT provides certain tools and contexts that books, or other tools, do not offer.

**4**  ICT encourages children to reach higher levels of thinking skills within a limited time – it also provides contexts for conceptual development and improved attitudes to science learning.

**5**  In primary schools in England and Wales (and throughout many other developed countries) there are a lot of ICT resources, because of the amount of money that has been spent in recent years. Many children also use complex ICT equipment and ideas in their homes. What a waste of a useful resource it would be if teachers did not make use of this in planning and carrying out their teaching.

## Why is ICT appropriate for education?

DfES (Department for Education and Skills) and NOF (New Opportunities Fund) training guidance (www.tta.gov.uk/teaching/ict/nof/nof.htm) suggest four functions of ICT that make it appropriate for education (although none of these is about motivating children or enjoying teaching and learning):

- speed and automatic function
- capacity and range
- provisionality
- interactivity

Speed and automatic function could include using databases to search and ask questions of many records in science experiments. Capacity and range might include the use of a CD-ROM or the Internet to gain scientific information. Provisionality suggests that data entered in word, graphics or numbers can easily be edited or altered, so a picture taken during a science investigation could be enhanced to show specific aspects of plant growth. Interactivity can be described in different ways – the interactivity of a child using an interactive whiteboard, or interacting with an Integrated Learning System, or using email to interact by communicating with someone else.

## 1.1 A creative approach to teaching and learning

### Why do we need a creative approach?

Research evidence about children's attitudes to science indicates that they are more interested in primary schools, but that this interest is reduced in secondary schools. Why? Recent research (Murphy and Beggs 2003) from Northern Ireland shows that the upper years in primary school are now also affected by this reduction of interest and the research suggests that the approach to science, with the emphasis on passing exams and tests, is responsible for this. What can be done? A more creative approach with more practical work for children and more relevance to everyday lives is one answer that seems to be gaining ground. The recent UK Government document, *Excellence and Enjoyment*, articulates several principles of learning and teaching, among them:

> Make learning vivid and real: develop understanding through enquiry, creativity, e-learning and group problem solving.

(DfES 2003: 29)

## What is creativity?

The QCA materials on 'Creativity: Find it, promote it' (http://www.ncaction.org.uk/creativity/index.htm) provide case studies on how teachers can promote creativity across all National Curriculum subjects. It gives examples of how promoting creativity can improve pupils' self-esteem, motivation and achievement. It also gives a definition of creativity as:

> First, they [the characteristics of creativity] always involve thinking or behaving *imaginatively*. Second, overall this imaginative activity is *purposeful*: that is, it is directed to achieving an objective. Third, these processes must generate something *original*. Fourth, the outcome must be of *value* in relation to the objective.

## How can creativity be promoted?

Ways for teachers to promote creativity are divided into sections, with examples given in each. The main sections for planning are:

- Set a clear purpose for pupils' work.
- Be clear about freedoms and constraints.
- Fire pupils' imagination through other learning and experiences.
- Give pupils opportunities to work together.

(http://www.ncaction.org.uk/creativity/promote.htm)

Then for promoting creativity while teaching:

- Establish criteria for success.
- Capitalise on unexpected learning opportunities.
- Ask open-ended questions and encourage critical reflection.
- Regularly review work in progress.

Creativity is addressed throughout this book in various ways that echo some of these ideas on the creativity website – some examples are given below (the sections in italics are reproduced from the creativity website).

## Chapter 4 Flight

'What makes a good parachute?' is a question that is asked in section 4.3 of this chapter.

*Help pupils to develop criteria that they can use to judge their own success, in particular, the originality and value of their work* (which can be as simple as asking, 'What makes a good …?').

## Chapter 6 Let there be light

Several ideas are suggested about collecting children's own thoughts, giving them opportunities to share the alternative ideas and then carry out investigations to find the answers to their questions.

*Be willing to stand back and not give all the answers but provide helpful prompts, if necessary.*

## Chapter 7 Science and technology in everyday life

Starting points for science and ICT teaching in the home, in the supermarket and through communication with real scientists are suggested.

*Use stimulating starting points such as artefacts, problems, stories with human interest, topical events.*

## Chapter 8 Energy

In a section on electricity within this chapter, you are shown how a student teacher used role play to help his pupils learn about the flow of electricity through a **circuit**.

*Use a range of learning styles, for example practical experimentation and problem solving, role play and dance, visual materials such as diagrams and cartoons, small group discussion and collaboration.*

## Chapter 9 'What if a chair was made of chocolate?' Materials and particles

Making a 'what if' book to share with others is one of the suggestions in this chapter. Children work together in groups and then record their ideas to show to others, using ICT tools to carry out this recording process.

*Plan for pupils to share their work with others; this tends to be very motivating. Ask questions such as 'What if …?', 'Why is …?' and 'How might you …?' to help pupils see things from different perspectives and come up with new ideas.*

## Chapter 10 Cells: 'What is grass made of?'

Children use their everyday experience of grass and ask questions about it in a science lesson and then explore answers from the Internet. Other children use the CD-ROM of *The Amazing Human Body* (Dorling Kindersley) which shows the insides of the body.

*Give pupils access to film, video and the Internet, which can help them to connect their learning to everyday experiences.*

## The Planet Science approach

Another recent publication, dealing with a creative approach to science, is *The little book of experiments* (Duncan and Bell 2002) from the Planet Science/Astra Zeneca project (www.planet-science.com). Although the experiments it contains are not necessarily new ideas, they are presented with interesting scenarios so that pupils will be drawn into thinking scientifically and will be trying to solve problems through the experiments they carry out. Some of the ideas are also more suited to Key Stage 3, with older children and more secondary school equipment.

## Other creative approaches

Another way of providing a more creative approach to teaching is to integrate a number of different subjects in a cross-curriculum ethos. This does have some problems, though, particularly in the possibility of dilution of more difficult subjects like science (Harlen 2000). A cross-curricular approach will only work if the learning objectives are clearly articulated and the science and ICT learning is assessed in a sensitive way. The QCA scheme adaptation (DfEE 2000) does provide suggestions for ways in which science contributes to the wider aims of primary education, especially in links with personal, social and health education (PSHE) and citizenship (see the website for more recent news and updates, http://www.qca.org.uk/ages3–14/).

## Creativity in investigations

Wenham makes some interesting points about creativity in science investigations – when we are looking for patterns in the results of our investigations, it requires a creative imagination to make sense of these. He proposes that science problem solving demands a combination of logical thinking and bright ideas, 'a synthesis between two apparently opposing qualities: creative imagination and strict criticism' (Wenham 1995: 5).

## 1.2  Big ideas in science – process skills and progression

## Science process skills

Science skills or science **process skills** are those skills that scientists are likely to use in many different contexts, in order to discover new knowledge or help explain events. In primary schools, we can identify such skills as:

- observation
- raising questions
- predicting
- hypothesising
- planning

- experimenting
- measuring
- presenting information
- drawing conclusions
- interpreting evidence
- communicating

> Scientific method is about developing and evaluating explanations through experimental evidence and modelling. This is a spur to critical and creative thought.
>
> (DfEE 1999: 76)

## Big ideas and research

Some of the big ideas in this section are based on those identified by Harlen (2000) in her book on *The Teaching of Science in Primary Schools*; others arise from the way the National Curriculum in science is structured, particularly in Key Stage 3. Some are drawn from a body of research in science education started by Piaget in 1929 (Atherton 2003 – see web links) with the publication of his work on children's ideas about the world. His research continues to the present day with workers in many countries contributing to the debate on how learning takes place and how teaching can best support children's learning. Various strands of research have contributed, with several now being termed 'constructivist'. (For fuller explanations of these theories see Chapter 2.) But the problem for a teacher or student teacher in a classroom is how to turn research findings into practical teaching lessons and sequences of lessons. This book attempts to show how this can be done.

## How can children make progress?

One of the most important ideas in teaching and learning is that we know children learn because they make progress in understanding, knowledge or skills. The idea of progression is a contested one.

Harlen discusses the problem of progression in ideas and how to describe it. She identifies three ways in which children can make progress:

1 Moving *from description to explanation*.
2 The development of generalisation, moving *from small to big ideas*, as in describing an animal and its likely home to generalising that animals of a particular type live in particular types of place.
3 *Sharing their ideas with others*, moving from a personal to a shared understanding.

## Moving from description to explanation

Essentially this means that children will at first be aware of things happening and will describe them as individual cases without linking them to any overall pattern. At a later stage in their development, or through interventions from teachers, they begin to notice that there are possible reasons for these things happening.

## Moving from small ideas to big ideas

A small idea can arise from a single experience and it builds into a bigger one when children are helped to link this to another small idea and build a bigger one from the juxtaposition. This relates to the concept of synergy – that the sum of two small ideas gives rise to a bigger one that is more than the simple addition of the two – the whole is bigger than the parts.

## Sharing their ideas with others

An important part of the science process is the need to share ideas and compare one idea with another. Children need to be supported in this by teachers organising time for discussions (see Chapter 12 for more on this theme).

## Prediction and hypothesis

Harlen then goes on to exemplify ideas about progression in a number of contexts, some of which are reflected in the cases described in this book. Her first point is linked to a common misunderstanding for many of us – the difference between prediction and hypothesis. A prediction is a guess at what you think will happen in a particular situation, e.g. I think that the football will bounce higher than the tennis ball. The hypothesis is an attempt to explain why you think something, in other words a hypothesis is an explanation, not just a description of an outcome. So the hypothesis might be that the football will bounce higher because it has more air in it and air is bouncier than solid objects. A prediction then applies to a single situation, while a hypothesis attempts to generalise into some kind of theory. Children may demonstrate their progress by bringing greater experience to bear on their predictions or by using more complex explanations.

## Continuity and progression

'Continuity' is a term often linked with progression, rather like hypothesis and prediction go together – the trouble is that their meanings can then become confused. Continuity refers to the process carried out by teachers in planning, so that children are offered sequences of activities that have some connections to each other. The teacher hopes that children will learn from these activities and hence make progress. So continuity is about what the teacher does and progress is what children make.

## What does 'progression' mean?

Progression of ideas seems to mean change in ideas towards some sort of notion of what is more scientific – but this depends on our own adult view of what is scientific. So to chart progression, a student teacher needs to have a clear understanding of scientific concepts, as well as basic knowledge. However, children make progress in many different ways and teachers may miss this progress if they adhere too closely to schemes of work that view progression in a different way. Sometimes children's ideas change in ways that may seem that they are going backwards (in relation to scientific understanding). Yet this would need to be recognised by the teacher as a kind of progress for the particular child. Progression is defined through the National Curriculum in terms of levels of attainment. In primary schools, children are supposed to develop their knowledge and investigative skills through five levels. These are exemplified by a set of statements, for example, in observation skills:

Level 1  Describe observation

Level 2  Make observations related to tasks

Level 3  Make relevant observations

Level 4  Make a series of observations adequate for tasks

Level 5  Observe and measure repeatedly and with precision

(Hollins and Whitby 2001: 13)

## Investigations or experiments

The idea of an investigation is very different from the traditional experiment that was a feature of many lessons in secondary schools, where children were required to prove certain things that had already been discovered by scientists in the past. In primary science, we should not ask children to carry out experiments of that type. This is partly because science cannot prove anything, in the way that maths can (look this up in books about the philosophy of science, if you are interested). But more important is the view of science education that requires children, as learners, to be actively engaged in the whole process of science, from asking the initial questions, through planning investigations to interpreting the results and communicating with others about their findings. They should be asking questions themselves and then trying to find out answers to these questions in the same ways as research scientists would, by carrying out an investigation to which they do not know the answer already. This notion of investigation is closely linked to the idea that children should not expect adults to give them the right answers, but that they should find answers through practical activities themselves. This is not to suggest that children can discover everything about the world. The role of the teacher is important in guiding children towards better ways of investigating as well as interpreting the evidence they collect.

## Types of investigation

Harlen (2000) identifies five different types of investigation, used in primary science. She categorises them as:

■ Information-seeking investigations, such as what happens when eggs hatch?

■ Comparing or fair testing, such as which is the better fertilizer for plants?

- Pattern finding, such as do taller trees have more tree rings?

- Hypothesis generating, such as why do echoes appear in some places?

- How-to-do-it investigations, such as how do you build a strong bridge model?

(Harlen 2000: 85–87)

She suggests that information-seeking investigations usually emphasise observation and communication skills, which may be more suitable for younger children, but that they may also lead to other types of investigation. An information-seeking investigation is suggested in Chapter 7, section 7.1, where children are asked to find out about different kinds of sugars. It leads on to another practical investigation involving the burning of sugars and comparing the results.

Comparison or fair-testing investigations are more useful if the children themselves are involved in making the decisions about the criteria, e.g. 'Which is best?' should lead to 'How do we define best?' Advantages of this type of investigation include the potential for identifying and controlling variables as well as finding out something new.

Pattern-finding investigations emphasise the interpretation of the results and lead children towards thinking about the concept of cause and effect. They are often well suited to the collection of larger amounts of data and hence the use of ICT tools such as databases and spreadsheets. In Chapter 4, the suggestion is made that children use a spreadsheet to record and look for patterns in data about parachutes.

Hypothesis-generating investigations attempt to find explanations for events and observations. The initial explanations should be subjected to further testing. Alternative hypotheses should also be considered. ICT can support this type of investigation by supporting the communication between children in their discussions of the alternative ideas, for example through word processing as a form of accurate presentation or through email to support communication over distance. In Chapter 5 there are some ideas about how children might use electronic mail to communicate with others about environmental and sustainability issues.

How-to-do-it investigations may also involve ICT since many technological problems arise in an information-rich context – an example in Chapter 7 is about how to control traffic lights.

## Variables in investigations

Science investigations are managed better if you can help children to identify the variables they need to consider. There are different types of variable that you have to think about in investigations. One type is the independent variable, another is the dependent variable, and then there are controlled variables (Wenham 1995: 12) and others which are not controlled, but which can be ignored as irrelevant. You would expect the colour of a toy car to be an irrelevant variable in an investigation of velocity down a ramp, but the colour would be a relevant variable in investigations on camouflage of the car. You might expect the colour of a crayon to be irrelevant in investigating the floating or sinking of the crayon, but actually we have found with some makes that the green crayons sink, while the black and red ones float. So here, colour is an important variable. Children need support in the ways in which they identify variables and how to treat them.

## 1.3  Big ideas in teaching science – content and concepts

### Reasons for choosing big ideas in science

The big ideas in science are in fact taken from the Key Stage 3 National Curriculum rationale and adapted in this book to the primary school context. It is likely that most children in the primary school would be unable to access the big ideas, but they should be learning the kinds of science ideas that will enable them to access these ideas later. So although we are not actually teaching the details of what cells are and their functions, we should be giving children background knowledge, skills, concepts and attitudes that will allow them to understand the more abstract ideas when they are taught. In the main subject-based chapters in this book, big ideas are approached and examples of how this is done are given below.

### Chapter 4 Flight

The discovery of flight by humans is an example of one of the most important scientific and technological advances since the wheel – although perhaps superseded by TV and communications now?

### Chapter 5 Sustainability and living things

The big idea in this chapter is that sustainability should be one of the principles underpinning education generally, not just primary education or teaching and learning about science and teaching and learning with ICT.

### Chapter 6 Let there be light

How we see is important, as vision is one of the most used and valued senses. The way in which light helps us to see is the big idea in this chapter.

### Chapter 7 Science and technology in everyday life

Learning in science is supposed to use everyday contexts so that children can see the connections between science at school and their own lives.

> Science stimulates and excites pupils' curiosity about phenomena and events in the world around them … Through science, pupils understand how major scientific ideas contribute to technological change – impacting on industry, business and medicine and improving quality of life.
>
> (DfEE 1999: 76)

## Chapter 8 Energy

The overarching concept or big idea in this chapter is **energy**. In one sense, you could argue that energy does not exist (do ideas exist as real things?) but is of extreme importance – wars are fought over energy resources – we should save energy. But science says you cannot use it up anyway. One of the problems is that the language we use in everyday life may have a different meaning to scientific language.

## Chapter 9 'What if a chair was made of chocolate?' Materials and particles

The big idea here is the existence of particles that are too small to see. It links with the big idea in teaching that we should try to make the imperceptible perceptible.

## Chapter 10 Cells: 'What is grass made of?'

The concept of a cell is too abstract for primary children, yet we need to lay foundations for later learning – but how? Some investigations are suggested in this chapter for dealing with living things, including ourselves.

## Chapter 11 Learning out of school

The big idea here is that children actually learn about science and ICT outside the classroom as well as within it. Teachers can plan to harness this learning by taking children outside the classroom, into the school grounds or outside the school completely into the local or more distant environment.

## 1.4 Big ideas for teaching through ICT

### What are the big teaching ideas with ICT?

The teacher can use ICT with the whole class or with small groups or individual children. For whole classes, a teacher might want to use ICT for:

- presentation of information
- demonstration of processes or skills
- explanation of concepts
- giving instructions
- linking concepts and ideas
- showing pictures with sounds
- presenting texts

### Presenting information

Information can be presented graphically to children through a variety of forms and styles, i.e. through pictures or diagrams, or through moving images, e.g. cartoons, videos, video clips. Information can be presented through the use of interactive whiteboards rather than blackboard/chalk, or whiteboard/pen. PowerPoint slides might be useful to present sequences of ideas and instructions, especially if they need to be presented several times. Some schools are co-operating to prepare and collect together resources using ICT that can be used across a number of classes or in subsequent years.

## Demonstrating processes or skills

Demonstrations would be useful in science, if you can find a CD-ROM or Internet site that shows specific teaching points, like the speeded-up sequence of plant growth or the process of **digestion** within the human body.

## Explanation of concepts

The explanatory power of ICT could support the teacher's explanations to help children understand how electrical circuits can be connected. Of course, children would need to use electrical components themselves, as well as comparing their ideas to those provided by others' explanations.

## Giving instructions

Using ICT can replace the need for handwritten lists or handouts. Instructions can be brought back more easily on screen than a set of instructions that has been erased from a whiteboard.

## Linking concepts and ideas

There are software tools (Inspiration, from TAG developments) that help teachers present concept maps that link ideas and concepts together. Although concept maps can be made using a blackboard, whiteboard or large piece of poster paper, the software allows you to save brainstormed concept maps and then retrieve them later to adapt or edit.

## Showing pictures with sounds

Many CD-ROMs use video clips operating through Quick-Time that show, for example, selected aspects of animal behaviour and the sounds associated with them. Internet sites also provide this kind of service, which is useful if the school has broadband access to the Internet. Most modern computers have libraries of pictures (clip art) and sound installed within them.

## Presenting texts

Text can be 'written up' on the whiteboard through computers linked to projectors or through interactive whiteboards. Children's own written outcomes can be displayed in this way or teachers' initial ideas presented and then altered during discussion with the children. Brainstorming can be presented and the results saved through this function of ICT.

But ICT is often used in the classroom both as a teaching and a learning tool. Data logging, for example, is both a teaching (demonstration) and learning (children actually logging the data) aspect of ICT (see section 1.5).

## Should children in primary schools be using computers?

There are obvious connections between the use of ICT and adult activities in jobs. But it is less obvious that children should be using ICT in primary schools, since most adults of a certain age did not use ICT in their own schooling, but have still managed to function in a computer age. Some countries avoid the use of ICT in primary schools because the philosophy is that young children should be doing different things from adults and that play and practical activities are more important than using computers. But the counter-argument is that children themselves are using computers at home already for both play and learning, so schools are echoing everyday life by also providing ICT. Another argument is that some children are disadvantaged if they do not have access to computers at home and that school may have a role to play in helping these children. In theory, children should be using computers in school to help them do things more easily and effectively, to allow them to achieve higher level skills and ideas.

## Teaching and learning with ICT

Examples of ICT purely as teaching tool occur in Chapter 3 with a student using an interactive whiteboard as a one-stop shop. Most examples in the book mix teaching and learning functions of ICT – a digital microscope, for example, is suggested in Chapter 5 as a whole-class teaching tool for showing children what minibeasts look like, or for the use of a small group or an individual child to study chosen features.

## Supporting ICT

Fox (2003) suggests supporting teaching by finding resources on the Internet, storing them and making them available to others who may be teaching a similar topic. This works both ways, of course. He also suggests saving differentiated worksheets, then modifying them by, for example, simplifying the text, reducing the content, increasing the point size (p. 85).

## The software available

It is obviously useful for a teacher to know what software is available in a school, for use with a particular class or age range. The software might be in the form of floppy disks, or CD-ROMs or programs installed on the classroom computers. It might be installed on a network available through passwords to particular year groups. Some software may be available through the Internet. Try carrying out an audit of the software available in one specific year group, using the format in Directed Activity 1.1.

**Directed Activity 1.1    A software audit**

| | |
|---|---|
| Software title | Title and company producing it |
| Age range | Is it for specific ages and linked to National Curriculum stages or for wider use? |
| Curriculum area | Is it just for science or can it be used for many different areas of curriculum? |
| Type of format | On a floppy, CD-ROM, the network, Internet, or zip drive? |
| Does it need peripheral devices? | For example, a microphone, sensor, printer or special drive? |
| Do I need special training? | Is it something that requires a study of the handbook or manual, or some apprenticeship training with an expert? |
| Is it for teacher or children to use? | Can a teacher use it through a projector, large screen or interactive whiteboard? Is it intended for individual children to use? |

## 1.5  Big ideas for learning through ICT

## What are the big ideas?

The National Curriculum for ICT presents a framework for the knowledge, skills and understanding that is contained in four aspects:

- Finding things out

- Developing ideas and making things happen

- Exchanging and sharing information

- Reviewing, modifying and evaluating work as it progresses

(DfEE 1999: 98–101)

Are there some big ideas that can help children to learn through ICT? One of the most important is to let the children explore different ways of doing things, without the need to worry that they may 'break' it. As long as the children are taught to save their outputs (or their work, if you want to look at it as work) then it is unlikely that they will damage anything beyond retrieval.

## Alternatives in ICT

One of the big ideas in ICT is that there is not necessarily just one right answer. There are often several different ways to carry out functions with a computer, although some devices need to be treated more carefully. Within the most common word processor, Word, there are several ways to carry out a function like deleting, such as deleting backwards one letter at a time using the backspace (arrowed) key, or using the delete forward key, or highlighting the text and pressing control X. So encouraging them to find alternative ways of doing things can enhance children's creativity. An experienced teacher, a deputy head and ICT co-ordinator, was surprised when the six-year-olds in his class discovered that a double click on the touch pad of the new laptops did the same as a left mouse click, followed by the enter key. As the technology changes, we should expect that children will sometimes discover new ways of carrying out some functions and then teach them to us.

## Data logging and science

One of the big ideas in ICT is that measuring things can be made much less time-consuming and that recording data can be quicker and more efficient. Data logging means both measuring and recording the data, such as light intensity, temperature or sound levels, through digital tools and computers. There are further ideas about how and when to use data loggers in subsequent chapters. However, children also need to experience some alternative ways of measuring and recording, so that they know which ways are most appropriate in different situations. There can be a similarity with writing in different ways – we might let children use a quill pen with ink as a historical lesson, or a fountain pen for more recent history, but since most people nowadays use some variety of ballpoint pen, pencil or computer for writing, do not insist that they continue to use old methods and techniques any longer. With ICT tools now readily available in everyday life as well as in schools, we should be showing children the variety of alternatives as well as asking them to use regularly the most appropriate tools.

## Good practice with ICT

NAACE (2002) (National Association of Advisors for Computers in Education) identify five key features of good practice with ICT:

- autonomy
- capability
- creativity
- quality
- scope

Autonomy means that children develop independence, take control of their learning and work independently.

Capability implies that they develop ICT skills appropriate to the tasks, apply them across different subjects to solve problems and make critical judgement about their uses of ICT.

Creativity is less clearly defined – it suggests exploration of different styles of communication, inspiration, innovation, use of multimedia tools to make presentations.

Quality is related to high standards of presentation, justifying the work they have done, taking pride in their outcomes, showing high expectations, concentration, persistence and determination as well as high quality thinking and analysis.

Scope means that ICT allows children to do things they would not be able to do in other ways, to interact with things and people outside the classroom or to think in new ways.

## Worksheets or pupil resources for children using ICT

Computer suites need more than just workstations; they should have desktop space for notes and pencil and paper. No office user with a computer on the desk would be without some space for paper too. Similarly in the classroom, the use of computers should be integrated into other work habits so children also need to have desktop or tabletop and paper and pencil space. A computer suite with only computers and no table space is a wasted resource. But there should be a variety of ways in which children are given instructions when using computers; sometimes they need paper-based resources; sometimes the instructions could be on an interactive whiteboard; sometimes the instructions could be verbal. They also need to be clear about how to record and save their responses; should this be on paper, or through files saved on the computer network or one of the drives?

## Integrating ICT within the classroom

One of the most difficult tasks that students and teachers seem to face in a normal classroom is integrating ICT into other subjects. So often, you forget to plan for the use of the one or two computers that are a normal part of the classroom furniture. Why is this? Too much emphasis on whole-class teaching? Not enough opportunity to explore the software in a school? (See Chapter 3 for case studies of teachers and student teachers using a variety of scenarios of computer and ICT tools, as well as Chapter 12 for some suggestions for deploying ICT tools in more effective ways.) It is a good idea in a science lesson to plan for a small group or two to use the classroom computer to support some aspect of the learning. This might be as an alternative to what the other children are doing, for example, using a word processor to complete a prediction sheet, instead of a paper prediction sheet, or using a database to enter the results of measuring lengths of children's arms, instead of paper and pencil records.

## Summary

In this chapter, you have read about creativity in general and in ways specific to science and ICT, about big ideas and how they appear in science content and in scientific process skills, as well as with teaching and learning with ICT. You should now be able to:

- Recognise some of the big ideas in science content and skills.

- Understand how to be a creative teacher.
- Use a variety of types of investigations.
- Know why ICT is important in supporting science teaching and learning.
- Recognise some of the ways of using ICT for teaching.
- Help children use ICT for learning.

## Web links

www.tta.gov.uk/teaching/ict/nof/nof.htm

www.dfes.gov.uk/primarydocument

http://www.qca.org.uk/ages3–14/

www.ncaction.org.uk

http://www.ncaction.org.uk/creativity/index.htm

http://www.ncaction.org.uk/creativity/promote.htm

www.planet-science.com

http://www.educate.org.uk

Atherton, J. S. (2003) *Learning and Teaching: Piaget's developmental psychology* [On-line] UK: Available: http://www.dmu.ac.uk/~jamesa/learning/piaget.htm.

NAACE (2002) *Implementing ICT* (see www.naace.org.uk).

# Theories of learning in science and ICT

## Introduction

This chapter provides a brief theoretical look at learning and teaching in primary schools. Although it is aimed mainly at teaching and learning science and ICT, it introduces some of the main ideas underpinning teaching and learning generally. It is not intended to provide any deep coverage of educational theory, but it does consider some of the implications of the teaching and learning theories. Among the theories the chapter does mention are behaviourism, active learning, multiple intelligences and social constructivism, with examples of how these theories can be put into practice in teaching science and ICT.

## Learning objectives

By the end of this chapter you should be able to:

■ Recognise the major learning theories in primary education.

■ Be aware of social constructivist principles underpinning science teaching.

■ Know about the ways in which ICT can support learning.

■ Recognise how teaching and learning in science and ICT are underpinned by learning theories.

## 2.1 General theories on teaching and learning

### Three main learning theories

Watkins (2003) provides a useful brief overview of three main views of learning:

■ Learning is 'being taught'.

■ Learning is 'individual sense-making'.

■ Learning is 'building knowledge as part of doing things with others'.

## 'Learning is being taught'

This view is based on behaviourist principles associated with Skinner (1950) and the view that you teach children by telling them things, showing them, and then reinforcing their memories and motivation with rewards. Although this may work with dogs, as Pavlov showed in the 1920s, humans have more complex brains and more complicated patterns of behaviour, hence this theory has lost ground in recent years. However, many early computer programs use 'drill and practice' exercises which echo the theory – tell the kids, then test them, reward them with a smiley face or friendly sound, punish them with a nasty noise.

You do still find echoes of behaviourism in the ways in which teachers provide external rewards and punishments in many classrooms – these often take the form of smiley badges and stickers, ticks on 'good behaviour' charts followed by 'golden time', or through defined stages in warnings for 'bad behaviour', like verbal or written warnings, reporting to head teacher or to parents. Positive praise for pupils is usually thought of as 'better than' telling off, but both could be seen as aspects of behaviourist theory in practice.

## 'Learning is individual sense-making'

The next major learning theory puts more attention on the learner and the processes that learners go through. It suggests that cognitive processes (or thinking skills) are important, rather than just remembering. It also stresses the emotional and social aspects of learning. Here learning is seen as an active not a passive process. In one sense, the advice to a learner that you need to read with a pencil in your hand is an example of this approach. The reader of any type of text needs to actively seek meaning in that text, and one way to do this is to respond to the text by making one's own notes or annotations. Although some critics in the popular press may dismiss 'learning as sense-making' as newfangled and lacking in rigour, it actually dates back to Socrates, around 400 BC. He used questioning to teach his students, implying that making them think about their own ideas was more important than giving them information. The theory is often categorised as active learning or constructivism.

## 'Learning is building knowledge as part of doing things with others'

The third main type of learning theory is sometimes known as 'social constructivism'. It suggests that knowledge at a higher level or 'meaning' is made by people interacting with others; a social rather than individual activity. Language, culture and communication are seen as necessary parts of the process of learning. Watkins (2003: 14) quotes a child learner to explain how this can work:

> You learn more if you explain to people what to do – you say things you wouldn't say to yourself really. So you learn things that you wouldn't know if you were just doing it by yourself.

## Multiple intelligences

Howard Gardner's views on intelligence have also recently become popular. He was Professor of Education at Harvard University when he developed the theory of multiple intelligences in 1983. The theory suggested that intelligence should not be seen as a single measurable feature of the human mind, but instead as (at least) eight alternative types of intelligence:

- linguistic intelligence ('word smart')
- logical-mathematical intelligence ('number/reasoning smart')
- spatial intelligence ('picture smart')
- bodily-kinaesthetic intelligence ('body smart')
- musical intelligence ('music smart')
- interpersonal intelligence ('people smart')
- intrapersonal intelligence ('self smart')
- naturalist intelligence ('nature smart')

## Teaching implications

One of the most important implications of this theory for teaching is the move away from the view that teaching is telling and learning is listening. 'Chalk and Talk' teaching styles are surprisingly still common in many primary classrooms and can be easily disguised with some of the newer learning technologies like interactive whiteboards (where their use may be far from interactive). If we think of the children as having a range of 'intelligences', then we should also plan our teaching to address this variety. Could chanting the times tables help children by engaging with their musical intelligence? Does role play about electricity help to link with kinaesthetic intelligence?

> The theory of multiple intelligences proposes a major transformation in the way our schools are run. It suggests that teachers be trained to present their lessons in a wide variety of ways using music, cooperative learning, art activities, role play, multimedia, field trips, inner reflection.
>
> (http://www.thomasarmstrong.com/multiple_intelligences.htm)

## Directed Activity 2.1    Thinking about your own learning

**Resources needed**
Just your own memories

**Specific questions raised**
How do you learn best?
Which things do you learn better in different ways?

**Background to the activity**
Think about your learning of a specific skill, as a child, like riding a bike. Think about how you learn a new skill now, such as embossing leather for a book cover.

**The activity**
Learn something new like the first five words of the Japanese numbers. First, find the Western characters from the Internet. How would you go about remembering them?

## 2.2  Teaching and learning in science

### Social constructivism

Probably the most popular theory underpinning the teaching of science in primary schools today is social constructivism. This theory arose from Piaget's ideas on children's learning about the world around them, first published in 1929 and 1930. Piaget can be studied with a number of educational texts (Donaldson 1984, Wood 1998) and websites (for example http://www.dmu.ac.uk/~jamesa/learning/piaget.htm). It also follows from theories developed by Vygotsky on the relationship between thought and language. Some of the implications from Vygotsky's theory for teachers are that you need to assess the child's existing knowledge, teachers should provide appropriately sequenced learning activities and teaching must lead development, not lag behind it. Constructivism, according to Hollins and Whitby (2001: 1) 'is a perception of the way in which learning takes place. Learning is an active process involving the selection and integration of information by the learner.' Learners construct concepts to explain what they see, hear and otherwise experience. Yet learners cannot construct skills; they need to develop such skills through being shown and then practising them (like the way to use a microscope). They cannot construct factual knowledge; they need to memorise facts. So constructivism can only be a part of the way in which learning takes place.

### Children's ideas

Harlen's model of learning (2000) suggests that we make sense of new experience and develop ideas to explain these experiences using both science process skills (see Chapter 1) and previous experience. Teachers attempt to help children to make sense of the world by asking them to consider whether their ideas fit the evidence, using process skills and reasoning. She stresses the importance of taking children's existing ideas seriously. One stage in teaching science should be asking children about their existing ideas and then probing these more deeply, for example:

'Where do you think electricity comes from?'

'Electricity comes from God.'

'How do you think God gets it to us?'

'He comes in the night when we are asleep and puts it in those big round things' [gas holder near the child's school] or 'It comes from the shop' or 'It comes from the water.'

Try suggesting further questions to follow up the second two ideas listed above.

## Being naturally scientific?

Hollins and Whitby (2001) emphasise the importance of helping children to develop, rather than learn, science process skills. They propose that children start to use scientific skills (before being taught anything about these skills) to make sense of the world at an early age and that by the time they enter the nursery school, they may have already ex-perienced ways of interacting with the world around them in an investigative way. But what happens when this 'natural curiosity-driven' learning is replaced by formalised instructional-driven learning in a school classroom, where the child is a member of a much larger group?

## Ability grouping and science

Pat Murphy (1999: 2–3) identified the trend towards ability grouping or setting in Key Stages 2 and 1. She thought this might be an outcome of the literacy and numeracy strategies. She questioned whether this is appropriate for science teaching. Pollard (1997) concluded that assessment structures may unwittingly be undermining positive dispositions towards learning. Davies (1995) conducted a study of children in primary schools and concluded that their self-esteem decreased in the two years of standard assessment testing, that is in Year 2 and Year 6, when children are seven or 11 years old.

## Collaborative work in science

Research by Christine Howe (1995) concludes that there is value in peer interaction as long as preconceptions among the children differ – random grouping is likely to achieve this, while ability grouping or setting is less likely to produce a variety of ideas from the children. Hence, mixed-ability grouping would be preferable within a constructivist theory of teaching and learning. However, you could argue that children have a variety of different sorts of intelligences and abilities and so no group is going to have children of the same prior experience and 'intelligence'.

## 2.3 Teaching and learning with ICT

### Pedagogy of ICT teaching

Moseley *et al.* (1999) conducted a survey of effective pedagogy of the uses of ICT, although focusing on literacy and numeracy in primary schools. Among the factors they found to be important were:

- clear identification of how ICT would be used to meet specific objectives within subjects in the curriculum;

- ensuring that pupils have adequate skills to achieve those subject-specific objectives;

- a planned match of pedagogy with the identified purpose of ICT activities and learning objectives;

- adequate access to, and intensity of use of, the necessary equipment by pupils and teachers.

They also found that certain types of teaching style are likely to be more effective in using ICT – these were styles that valued collaborative working, enquiry and decision-making by pupils – in other words, a teacher who values a constructive approach to science teaching is also likely to use ICT more effectively.

The research team found that few teachers planned specific ways in which ICT contributed to subject teaching, although most teachers who used ICT did plan for specific IT capability. Another finding was that much computer use in the classroom was planned as an addition to the curriculum rather than as a key teaching strategy. An implication of the research was that teachers should consider a range of strategies to meet teaching objectives, such as using ICT for direct instruction in some cases. More focus was needed to gain the best results from the use of ICT. Children also have to be taught how to use the software or technology before they can make effective use of ICT, they suggest. For example, in a science investigation, this would mean that if pupils were being asked to use data-logging software to measure and record temperature changes over a certain time, they would first need to be taught directly how to use the equipment before engaging in the scientific learning. So a teacher trying to integrate ICT with science teaching would need to teach the ICT skills and techniques first. An alternative view would be that children would learn the ICT better if they had a task that demanded the use of these skills; so learning the skills in context would be likely to lead to longer lasting learning.

### A literature review

Mosely *et al.* also conducted a review of the literature in effective pedagogy and provided some important general principles:

- Teachers' beliefs and pedagogical purposes behind certain classroom practices are more important than the forms of the practices themselves.

- The most effective and efficient teaching strategies are made by balancing the needs of the majority and the particular needs of individuals within the class. (Differentiation in planning sessions should also be at the level of ICT uses – implication may be some children need computers at certain times more than others.)

- Teachers need something called pedagogical content knowledge, which involves knowledge and understanding of both subject and children – the preconceptions that children have as well as an understanding of what makes some aspects of a subject difficult, and ways of representing the ideas, powerful analogies, illustrations, examples, explanations and demonstrations.

- Effective teaching depends on lesson clarity, for example, using relatively straightforward sentences; avoiding vague, ambiguous or indefinite language; instructional variety; teacher task orientation; engagement in the learning process; and pupil success rate.

## Types of learning theory

Fox (2003) discusses three types of learning theory that have influenced teaching with ICT – he calls these (after Taylor 1980) computer as tutor, tutee or tool.

'Computer as tutor' is based on the behaviourist theory of Skinner, popular in the mid-1960s and still in evidence in some forms of computer programs, particularly ILS types (Integrated Learning Systems). Much of the so-called educational software designed for the home market falls into this category, with the computer as a teaching machine. However, the research suggests that the greatest progress happens when an adult mediates the ILS, rather than the children working through programs alone. But many teachers do use ILS programs and many children seem to enjoy them. Is motivation of children a sufficient reason for adopting this type of teaching tool?

'Computer as tutee' owes a great deal to the work of Papert (1980) who developed a language called LOGO. Using this language, children learn how to instruct the computer and other programmable tools (like Roamers and Pixies). In doing so, children learn that computers allow them to enter a world of thinking. So in this theory, children are learning by teaching computers, rather than in the first theory, where computers are teaching children.

Fox's third model, the 'computer as tool', follows a social constructivist theory, in which the computer allows children to learn other things, not about computers and ICT, but about other subjects. The computer is seen as a type of scaffolding, in Vygotskian language, which enables children to learn skills, develop ideas and acquire knowledge, which otherwise they would find difficult.

But in the busy atmosphere of the primary school, should we really be looking at the ways in which ICT use overlaps with all three of these theories? Should we also be looking at the reality of the ICT provision in schools and seeing whether the theoretical approaches outlined above have any bearing on current practice? One change of significance in recent years has been the introduction into primary schools of interactive whiteboards, both in normal classrooms and into computer suites. These tools have the potential to integrate a number of ICT functions, programs and teaching methods.

## Interactive whiteboards

An influential group in the UK that commissions and collates evidence about the influence of ICT on teaching and learning is BECTa (British Education, Communication and Technology agency). BECTa (www.becta.org.uk/research) looked at a number of ways of using interactive whiteboards, such as:

> Web-based resources for whole class teaching [see Chapter 3, case study 1 on the use of Spark-Island in a Year 4 class], showing video clips to help explain concepts, demonstrating software, presenting students' work to the rest of the class, creating digital flipcharts, manipulating text and practising handwriting, saving notes from the board for future use for quick and seamless revision.

They also identified key benefits:

- Encourages more varied creative and seamless teaching materials.
- Engages students to a greater extent than conventional whole-class teaching, increasing enjoyment and motivation.
- Facilitates student participation through the ability to interact with materials on the board.

Other useful material from BECTa includes a bibliography of research and articles about interactive whiteboards. This suggests that whiteboards inspire teachers to change their pedagogy and use more ICT, encouraging professional development. It seems that if a student teacher or any teacher has to use an interactive whiteboard, because there is no alternative in the classroom such as a normal white- or blackboard, then they are much more likely to use other ICT applications. The interactive whiteboard acts as a platform on which a number of other ICT applications are facilitated.

But the novelty does soon wear off so a range of approaches is necessary to maintain interest. Glover and Miller (2001) identify three levels of whiteboard use:

- To increase efficiency by using several ICT resources without disruption or loss of pace.
- To extend learning, using more engaging materials to explain concepts.
- To transform learning, creating new learning styles by interaction with the whiteboard.

## Levels of interactive whiteboard use

Another way of looking at levels of teaching and learning with interactive whiteboards was provided through a TTA workshop (November 2003) – five levels of use in a much simpler model:

- Use it as an ordinary screen for showing video or still images or texts.
- Use it to display a computer screen, through a data projector.
- Use it as an interactive board, using SMART board software like the notebook function.
- Use a mixture of computer screen and whiteboard functions.
- Transform the teaching and learning by fully integrating it into all lesson plans.

## Tablet PCs

BECTa also suggest that further research is needed, since the technology is so new, and identify Tablet PCs as another alternative to interactive whiteboards.

In primary schools and especially with younger children, the advantages of the boards can be that pupils do not have to use a keyboard to engage with the technology, so there is increased access for younger children (Goodison 2002).

Some teachers appreciate the power of interactivity inherent in these boards: 'As soon as I saw what was going on to the screen, I realised that I could respond to the differing visual and auditory learning strengths of the group' (Glover and Miller 2001: 263).

## Primary schools and interactive whiteboards

Penny McBroom is a primary school teacher who used interactive whiteboard technology along with digital cameras to help children to record images from their visit to a museum. They subsequently produced a class book and published this on the Web, using the handwriting lines part of the whiteboard software. Further ICT was used to link the class to American children in a study of the materials commonly used in the construction of their homes, so enabling children to explore the different reasons for using wood or clay in buildings (see Chapter 10 for children exploring materials used in the construction of their school). National Curriculum science for Key Stage 1 requires that children 'find out about the uses of a variety of materials (for example, glass, wood, wool) and how these are chosen for specific uses on the basis of their simple properties' (DfEE 1999: 80). But teachers also demonstrate a critical approach to some of the newer technology: 'There is some concern that we put ourselves in the position where we have to produce media rather than lessons' (Glover and Miller 2001: 265).

## Misconceptions in ICT

Misconceptions in ICT can be identified, but they are often different from misconceptions in science, as they be more related to errors in skills than in concepts. Look at the selection below and see if you recognise any and can sort them into skill or concept errors. The list originated from the website www.mirandanet.ac.uk.

1  Saving to A drive versus hard drive versus network drive – children need to know where they are saving their work so they can retrieve it later – usually this will be to a place on the school network, within their own class folder. Most primary school networks are based on this sort of system, but some may be more complex – it depends on how the children log on to the computer, as their own personal user name and password, or via a class user name/identity. The implication about saving to the network is that children do not have to return to the same computer again to retrieve their work, but can do it from any computer in the network. This is different from most children's experience of computers at home and may also differ from teachers' uses of home and college or school computer.

2  Word processing – using the caps lock to write capital letters rather than the shift key. Is this a misconception or just a lack of skill?

3  Deleting all the way back to a spelling error, rather than moving the cursor to the error and just changing the problem word. Children may not realise that the line of print can be entered at any place, but think that because they have written it in a linear way, then it can only be edited in the reverse of this linear fashion. Perhaps this is an example of the Piagetian idea of egocentricity?

4  Understanding the way in which a database manages to organise the information you put into it. Databases are not word processors. There are several different ways in which databases work, usually explained through metaphors like that of a branching tree.

5  When using the Roamer, the most common misconception is about the angles of an equilateral triangle – this is almost always found in adults using the Roamer for the first time – thinking that an angle of 60 degrees turn will make the Roamer create a triangle, whereas it requires a turn of 120 degrees to create an internal angle of 60 degrees.

6  Using LOGO on screen also produces misconceptions about which way to turn, so that if the screen turtle is pointing downwards, it would look as though a left turn is really a right turn.

7  The idea that editing a file is the same as saving it. Some programs automatically save the file – this only happens with a database file, not with a word-processed file.

Are these really misconceptions in the same way that science labels them, or are they more about the differences between children's thinking and that of the teacher, software designer or educational community? Are there any unifying conceptions in ICT in the first place (see www.mirandanet.ac.uk/profdev/misconceptions.htm)?

## Integrated learning systems

However, as with all research in education or elsewhere, it is likely that the results of the research are affected to some extent by the beliefs of the researchers themselves. A research group with different assumptions might have come up with a different style of research and different results. An example of this is the research on the effectiveness of interactive learning systems. These are programs that instruct pupils in specific skills, such as maths techniques, and are very popular with some teachers and children. The computer itself conducts both the teaching and the assessment of pupils and records the progress they make. Underwood and Brown (1997) have conducted extensive research into these types of programs and have shown that they also have value in helping certain children make measurable progress. So whatever kind of research you read has to be considered within its own research paradigm and can never be taken to apply to all pupils in all situations. Another problem with research into the uses of ICT is how rapidly ICT skills change. Research carried out on teachers' skills in 1999 suggested that they were less skilled in using search engines on the Web than in redrafting text. Research carried out in 2004 would be likely to reverse this and research into teachers' uses of texting would not even have been possible in 1999.

## 2.4 Science and ICT together

### Interactive whiteboards and science teaching

There are several ways that interactive whiteboards can be used in science teaching in the primary school. A teacher could save the results of children's brainstorming of ideas, which can be quickly written up on the board during an introduction or a plenary section of a lesson, so that they can be reminded of where they were when they start the next section or lesson. Lesson plans and resources to use with interactive whiteboards can be downloaded from the Internet, to support science lessons, but you have to be wary of just using these without some consideration of the underlying philosophy. Do they aim to just replace a book and provide passive learning situations or are they intended to be really interactive with the children as well as with the teacher?

### Low level skills and ICT

Twining in 'Viewpoint' from *Primary Science Review* (1999) examines the ways in which ICT can support science teaching and learning and concludes that ICT can reduce the amount of time that children need to spend on 'lower level' activities. He also identifies simulations and classifying through databases as potential links between science and ICT. In the context of collecting data on the rate of cooling of water inside different containers, for example, children could be using sensors that automatically record the temperature of the water at pre-selected intervals. Yet you could also argue that the measuring of temperature with a non-digital thermometer is an important skill, which should not be ignored or relegated to the category of low level, unless the children are engaged in some higher level activity in the time that they would normally be using the thermometers. What would they do instead? Of course, children should have access to data logging equipment at some stage in their scientific learning, but they should also experience the ideas and skills involved in measuring in the old-fashioned way. At some stage, children should be encouraged to reflect on the most appropriate tools for the task and to choose for themselves which type of equipment is more suitable. The problem for a teacher is to use the available equipment appropriately to support the learning of individual children, not just to achieve a quicker or more accurate experimental result.

## Pedagogy and time in the primary classroom

Frost (2002) suggests the use of simulations to enhance science learning, such as 'Exploring Science' for the Macintosh computer, from Granada software. Simulations can be useful because of the time limits of science investigations. So the germination of a seed – traditionally explored by children planting seeds and putting them in different places to check the effects of the environment on germination – can be done through computer simulations. Twining (1999) also suggests that simulations should supplement rather than replace practical activities. Seed germination and subsequent growing of plants are necessary activities and can be fitted relatively easily into the pattern of the school day and week, rather than seeing these activities as being part of a specific science lesson. The primary school day and week are very different from that in a secondary school, with its 50-minute lesson blocks in different rooms and labs. Most primary school children spend most of their time in the same classroom and most primary classes are run by a single class teacher who has opportunities throughout the day to carry out small tasks like encouraging children to check on plant growth, water plants, measure temperatures, and to record and discuss the changes. ICT as a tool rather than as a tutor or tutee is the theoretical model for this type of implementation, although you could use some types of simulation as a tool for teaching rather than learning – the computer as tutor model – if the simulation was the only way of approaching the topic.

## Classifying skills in science and ICT

There are several databases specially developed for primary school children, utilising either branching key or field type. A third idea from Twining is about classifying – obviously a science skill that can be supported through ICT. The problem again is about real objects and pictures of objects, but ICT can also be used here as a structure to help children sorting – almost a replacement for an adult. This reduces the pressure on children as well as the time provided by a busy teacher to each child. Again, this is a useful way to see ICT supporting science if the teacher then uses this saved time for another equally important purpose, not just interacting with a computer herself or instead of interacting with a child.

## Summary

In this chapter, you have been introduced to some general theories of teaching and learning, looked at the application of learning theories to the organisation and management of science teaching, explored some of the theoretical underpinning of ICT teaching in primary schools and seen how ICT can be linked with science teaching. You should now be able to:

- Recognise the main features of learning theories that underpin primary school teaching.
- Use the theoretical ideas from social constructivism and multiple intelligences when organising children into groups and classes to investigate scientific concepts.
- Understand how computers and other ICT equipment can be used as tutors, tutees or tools to support children's learning in classrooms, computer suites or outside the school.
- Make decisions about the relevance of and justification for using ICT tools to support science teaching and learning.
- Find further sources of research and theories about education.

## Web links

www.becta.org.uk/research

A site concerning research into ICT and its educational uses – particularly interesting is the section on 'What the research says' – a set of pdf files each of four pages, showing current research in specific areas of ICT education.

http://psychclassics.yorku.ca/Skinner/Theories/

www.ictadvice.org.uk

Advice from BECTa on doing ICT in classrooms.

www.hcrc.ed.ac.uk/Site/bibliographyrecent.html

A complex bibliography of research references on communication theories.

http://www.dmu.ac.uk/~jamesa/learning/piaget.htm

Some lecture notes about Piaget and his learning theories.

www.mirandanet.ac.uk/profdev/misconceptions.htm

An idiosyncratic article about misconceptions concerning IT, some jokey, some serious.

http://www.dur.ac.uk/elizabeth.meins/lect3.htm

A lecturer from the University of Durham has put her lecture notes about Vygotsky's theories on the Web at this site.

http://www.indiana.edu/~eric_rec/ieo/bibs/multiple.html

This site lists the results of an ERIC search about multiple intelligences. It gives references to academic articles and the abstracts of these articles.

http://www.thomasarmstrong.com/multiple_intelligences.htm

A site that gives useful information about the theory of multiple intelligences.

# 3

# Case studies from partnership schools

## Introduction

The examples in this chapter are taken from student and newly qualified teachers working in partnership schools. It demonstrates how they have managed to link science and ICT together in their teaching. Teaching plans and notes about the teaching are featured. None of the case studies is intended to be a perfect lesson and none is described exactly as it took place. Some additions have been made and in other places, elements of the lessons have been left out. The examples are included here to ground the rest of the contents of the book in reality. Partnership schools are schools that have a long-standing link with London South Bank University, in the sense that they often take our students for teaching practice and they may also provide employment for students after they qualify.

## Learning objectives

By the end of this chapter you should be able to understand how student and newly qualified teachers have:

- Taught about light and shadows – using interactive whiteboards and digital cameras.
- Used a computer suite – using Internet resources for science about keeping healthy.
- Explored outdoor areas for animal and plant life – using digital equipment.
- Planned science lessons – using laptops and other ICT tools in the classroom.

**TABLE 3.1    ICT National Curriculum links**

|  | Key Stage 1 (ages 5–7) | Key Stage 2 (ages 8–11) |
|---|---|---|
| Teaching about light and shadows | 1a, 5b | 5a, 5c |
| Using computer suites for science teaching | 3a, 5b | 1a, 5a |
| Using outdoor areas with digital equipment | 1a, 5b | 1b, 2b, 5b |
| Using laptops in the primary school | 1a, 3a | 1b, 2a, 3a, 5a |

**TABLE 3.2    QCA scheme links**

|  | Science | ICT |
|---|---|---|
| Teaching about light and shadows | 1D, 3F, 5E | 1C, 2C, 5F |
| Using computer suites for science teaching | 2A, 5A | 2C, 6D |
| Using outdoor areas with digital equipment | 2B, 4B, 5/6H | 1C, 2B |
| Using laptops in the primary school | 2A, 3B, 4A, 5A, 6A | 1B, 2C, 3B, 5D |

## What big ideas are in this chapter?

The reason for including this chapter is to ground the book in realistic situations, real classrooms where real student teachers are practising their skills. The big ideas from ICT are that you can use the various technologies for either teaching or for learning, or indeed for both, but that you need to be clear about what ICT is being used and why. Teaching with ICT means that you, the teacher, are using the technologies, whereas learning with ICT means that the pupils are using the technologies. Both are, of course, useful and important, but sometimes they are confused. In the four case studies described here, there is a mixture of teaching and learning with ICT.

## Case studies

Although none of the classrooms is described in detail and none of the lessons was carried out exactly as described here, the flavour of the cases is captured. Many other books on primary practice use a similar approach, describing case studies (Littledyke, Ross and Lakin 2000) or cameos (Cook and Finlayson 1999). Acknowledgements have been made at the start of the book to the specific schools and students who agreed to help with this chapter, but I have tried to make it impossible for any one case study to be clearly identified as having its origin in one situation. Perhaps student teachers reading this will recognise some of the similarities to the schools where they find themselves teaching? So this chapter shows what schools (in and around London) are like and how student teachers can make the best of the various settings.

## Setting, context and environment

The way in which the case studies are described relies on a constructivist or socio-cultural view of learning, which sees learning as embedded in layers of setting, context and environment (see Chapter 2 for teaching and learning theories). The differences between setting, context and environment are described in Cook and Finlayson (1999). They see 'setting' as the physical space occupied by the teacher and children, so it includes the size of the room, the computers in it, black- or whiteboards, projectors, the desks and tables, and other furniture. 'Context' is partly determined by the curriculum aspects of the learning. So the context would depend on the learning objectives of the lesson as determined by the parts of the National Curriculum being used as a guide to the teaching and learning. Context is also affected by the social and intellectual abilities of the children, but I have only mentioned these in passing in the case studies below. Finally 'environment' is defined as the classroom rules and procedures, a level of talk, formality and movement accepted as normal by the teacher and the children. Some might describe this as the classroom climate or ethos of the class. This last idea is one that student teachers may have most difficulty in changing, especially in a short period in a new class.

## 3.1  Teaching about light and shadows

### School ethos and student teacher environment

The school had some unusual methods and routines and used a variety of non-standard practices, which have their origins in positive discipline methodology. Children are quite used to moving to different classrooms for maths and English and expect to be

**TABLE 3.3** Setting for light and shadows lesson

| |
|---|
| **Setting** The classroom was equipped with an interactive whiteboard with the projector permanently mounted in the ceiling. The student and class teacher were expected to use it for most whole-class sessions, since it was at the front of the room, most of the children were facing that way and there was no alternative white- or blackboard. |
| **Context** The learning outcomes of the lesson were taken from the Science National Curriculum:<br>■ To understand that shadows will be the shape of objects blocking the light.<br>■ To understand that shadows change in length during the day.<br>■ To draw conclusions and tabulate the path of the sun through length and time. |
| **Environment** Children sat in formal rows facing the front of the class. Most of the time, children were expected to remain silent when seated unless the teacher gave them instructions to talk. They were out of their seats and discussing freely for a small part of this lesson, while they looked at the digital photos on the walls of the classroom. |

grouped according to different abilities in these lessons. Some teachers use kinaesthetic techniques that recognise children's needs for movement, good posture, good breathing, fresh air and water. Techniques like 'Think, pair and share' are regularly used so that children learn to co-operate and discuss questions, rather than accept a teacher's right or wrong judgement. This situation can be difficult for student teachers to manage, since the organisation is more complex than just one class with one class teacher.

## Learning objectives, aims and outcomes

The main learning objective for the lesson was displayed on the interactive whiteboard – a science one in fact, as the ICT in this case was all used in support of the teacher's role, not by children:

We are going to learn how shadows change during the day.

In her lesson plan, the student teacher had written three intended learning objectives:

a. To understand that shadows will be the shape of objects blocking the light.
b. To understand that shadows change in length during the day.
c. To draw conclusions and tabulate the path of the sun through length and time.

In the SPACE research (Osborne, Smith, Black and Meadows 1994), we were also concerned about the apparent height of the sun in the sky and the effect of this on the direction of the shadow. Would this be an aim for a subsequent lesson with these children? Is there a difference between learning objectives, learning outcomes and aims? Yes – an aim would be to teach the children about light and shadows – the learning objectives would be that they should be able to achieve a, b and c above; the learning outcomes would be what individual children achieved and these should be recorded by the student teacher in her own learning outcome checklist.

## Using a digital camera

The digital camera was used to take photos of some playground structures at five different times during the previous day (fortunately it had been fairly sunny all day). These five photos were pinned up in different places around the classroom walls, labelled A to E. Children were organised into pairs; each was encouraged to go and look at the pictures and see which they thought was the longest shadow and put them in order. The student gave them a clue and told them that C was the first. Eventually one pair was encouraged to think this through, got a ruler and measured the shadows more accurately. 'Think, pair and share' is a research-based technique, described in Chapter 12, which this school used frequently in many different lesson contexts. The student teacher also used it to provide the pairs of children with some opportunities to discuss ideas about the shadows and the apparent position of the sun. It provides excellent support for science in terms of encouraging children to communicate and to explore alternatives. A more experienced teacher would have used the Think, pair and share discussions as an opportunity to assess the ideas and record some of the misconceptions of certain children.

## Balancing pace with children's own ideas

Even experienced teachers would find it hard to maintain a balance between following up children's own ideas and misconceptions, with the need to keep up the pace of the lesson. One child, for example, noticed that the shadows in one photo were much less bright than in all the others and seemed to think this was an indication of the time of the day. In a sense he was right, because he knew that the day had become cloudier in the afternoon. But it was not relevant to the learning objective of the lesson, that shadows change in length during the day, so the student teacher did not follow it up. To have done so would have been good for the scientific learning of that child, but might have caused control problems if other children were not interested in this idea at this time.

## Integrating the Internet with the interactive whiteboard

She also used the Internet to download a video clip from http://www.sparkisland.com/ to demonstrate the 'apparent movement of the sun across the sky' and finally, during the plenary section, she used a word and number bank to help children reorganise shadow lengths and times in the day – four examples of ICT to support science teaching in a one-hour lesson.

## Extension ideas

- One extension activity, perhaps in the next lesson or with a group working with a learning assistant, would be to go out into the playground and measure the actual shadows.

- Another extension might be to use a compass and see where the sun was at different times in the day. This would support the Spark Island focus on learning about east and west.

- To assess the learning better, you could ask the children to draw something for themselves, such as objects and the shadows they think would be cast.

- To use interactive whiteboard for writing up the three main ideas emerging from the children's ideas about the lesson (i.e. darker/lighter, longer/shorter, east/west) and then ask the children to discuss them – and link this to the Spark Island 'where is the sun' quiz.

## 3.2 Using computer suites for science teaching

The computer suite is becoming a more common item in primary schools and many student teachers are finding that they have to use the room and equipment for the first time. Some may have a teacher's computer that can override the screen of the children.

**TABLE 3.4** Setting for computer suite

| |
|---|
| **Setting** Computer suites come in many shapes and sizes (see Chapter 7 for further explorations) but in this case study it had 15 computers, networked together, two printers, a whiteboard and table-mounted projector. There was also a carpet area where children could be gathered together away from the computer screens. |
| **Context** The main teaching objectives included both science and ICT. Science objectives were about health, including a balanced diet, the importance of exercise and healthy teeth. ICT objectives included being able to use a browser to search the Internet and extract relevant information. |
| **Environment** Children are expected to work individually or in pairs most of the time, although questioning is encouraged at the start and during the plenary. Some children will ask neighbours for help at times. Pairs may alternate control of the keyboard or mouse. Children will remain in same places during the lesson, but may move for the introduction and plenary, if there is space to gather together. |

There are particular issues that a teacher needs to consider when using a computer suite for science:

- Logging on to the system, using passwords.
- Retrieving previously saved items.
- How to save children's drafts to specific areas of the network?
- How to operate the printers?
- How to introduce the lesson when children are already seated at the computers?
- How to monitor and control the activities of children during the lesson?
- How to assess the learning that takes place when pairs of children are sharing a computer?
- How to organise the space to suit the science activity?
- How to follow up the lesson in the normal classroom?

## The Internet and science learning

There are some common ways in which computer suites are used for science – one of these is searching the Internet for specific information related to science teaching and learning. The main problem that arises is that although there is plenty of information on the Internet, very little of it is in a form suitable for primary school children to extract and understand. So just searching is usually a waste of time. Teachers need to find suitable sources of information before the start of the lesson, rather than relying on children being able to do this.

## Browsing a website

In one lesson I observed in a computer suite, the main focus was on information about being and keeping healthy. The children (aged 9–11 years) were encouraged to browse through information on the BBC site. The student teacher introduced the lesson and reviewed the main teaching objectives in terms of science and ICT. One of the pairs of children logged on to their machines within the school network environment. The student teacher gave instructions about the tasks to be undertaken and the amount of time available. Children then worked in pairs at their tasks. The first site they looked at was http://www.bbc.co.uk/learning/ and then they moved to a variety of others, such as http://www.bbc.co.uk/schools/revisewise/science/living/04_act.shtml. They had to extract what they thought was relevant, rather than focus on a particular aspect of health, such as healthy diet, the importance of exercise or healthy teeth. This way, the student hoped they would collect a variety of information, rather than all looking at the same issues.

## Some outcomes from the lesson

Few of the children understood the word 'browser' or that they were leaving the school intranet and using information from other places. This might be an objective in a subsequent lesson. The children were expected to search the chosen site, read or skim read for information in order to answer specific questions. Many of them found this more difficult than finding the information in a book, as they had done the previous week. The children who used computers a lot at home were better at finding and recording the information from the Internet than those without access to computers at home.

## 3.3 Using outdoor areas with digital equipment

## Previous teaching in this series

In previous lessons, the student teacher recorded that these six- and seven-year-old children had learnt about how plants reproduce and what they need to survive. They had shown interest in seeds and some had brought examples of plants and seeds into the

**TABLE 3.5** Setting for outdoor areas

| |
|---|
| **Setting** This was a school on the outskirts of London, serving a mixed community in terms of ethnicity. The outdoor areas are extensive for a London school, containing tarmac playgrounds, grassy areas and flowerbeds, a grass playing field and some rough grass edges. |
| **Context** There were two science objectives from the National Curriculum for the whole class:<br>■ Make observations and comparisons of local plants.<br>■ Observe and make records of animals and plants found.<br>■ Some children also learnt how to use the digital camera. |
| **Environment** In the classroom, there are formal rules about talking when sitting on the carpet or at desks, but outdoors these rules were somewhat relaxed during the observation periods. Movement was also allowed, but children were told to stay with their partner and also with the group supervised by one of the three adults. |

classroom. A previous lesson's learning had been differentiated so that two groups had started an experiment on germination and found that the conditions for this are different from those needed for plant growth. The student also recorded that some other groups needed to think about the use of scientific vocabulary to describe what they could see. Examples of this were 'stinking nettles' for stinging nettles, and use of the shortened word 'puter' for computer, which was then confused with the object called a pooter, which was used for collecting small animals like ants. Some children identified the pooter as a 'suck thing'.

## Planning for children's needs

A general objective for the next lesson was to enable the children to record what they could actually find in the local environment. One of the signs that a teacher is planning well is that she can record the needs of the children in the evaluation of one lesson and then include these needs in her planning for a subsequent lesson.

## Using ICT equipment for measuring and recording

The ICT equipment that was used in the example was a digital camera, which helped the children to carry out a learning objective – to record the plants and animals found. They could also have used digital thermometers to record the differences in temperature in shady and open areas of the playground and the surrounding bushes and grassy areas. Some of them could then have used this information to make connections between this data and the types of animals and plants found in the different locations. Since the children were trying to identify what sort of habitats plants grow in, and they had discussed the conditions for plant survival in a previous lesson, they could have used a light meter to measure the amount of light in the places they found different plants and animals. If the equipment had been available, they could also have used data logging to measure and record environmental conditions over a longer period of time.

## Planning for other adults

The problem faced by a student in a six-week practice is that it takes a long time to gain the confidence and techniques to manage a class in an outdoor area and then to gather all the necessary equipment to integrate ICT with the science. A solution that she did use to help in this process was to plan carefully for the use of two other adults – both the class teacher and the learning support assistant took charge of groups in the outdoor areas.

## 3.4  Using laptops in the primary school

**TABLE 3.6**  Setting for laptops

| |
|---|
| **Setting** This was a small primary school (one form entry) in an inner London Borough. It was built about 150 years ago and has very small classrooms, with high windows and no corridors. Teachers and children have to walk through some classrooms to reach their own rooms, so the school can be very noisy. All classes are equipped with two or three PCs and all can have access to up to six laptops, using wireless (radio) links to the central broadband network. |
| **Context** The contexts vary in the case studies described below. Some have science learning objectives; others include ICT teaching tools or ICT learning objectives. |
| **Environment** The school has a definite Christian ethos and is on the same site as the church. Children wear school uniforms. Most classes use similar systems of rewards and punishments, with points awarded for good behaviour on an individual and group basis and a period called Golden Time each week, when children who have achieved good behaviour targets can choose their own activities. |

## Why choose laptops in a primary school?

The school made a decision to buy laptop computers because of the limitations of size – there was no space for a computer suite and very little space within the classrooms for more computers either. But they also decided that laptops would allow the ICT to be integrated into teaching and learning much more easily than a computer suite. So they bought an initial set of 15 laptops and equipped them with wireless transmitters, intending to use them all in one classroom with all the children (in pairs). However, this did not work well and caused too much disruption, so the decision was made to spread the machines out in smaller numbers. Each classroom can now have six laptops as well as three stand-alone PCs. Most classrooms are also equipped with a ceiling mounted projector and some also have interactive whiteboards. One class in which the laptops are not used any longer is Reception, with children aged four and five years. These children do use PCs, equipped with mouse controls, as well as a variety of other ICT tools like Roamers, but they found the touchpad controls of the laptops too difficult.

## A Training School

Part of the funding for these resources came from the Teacher Training Agency through a scheme called 'Training Schools'. Hence it has student teachers throughout the year working in many of the classes, as well as hosting larger groups of student teachers for short visits to work with children and computers. Some examples of the ways in which teachers and children are using the laptops in science are given below.

## Spreadsheets and pulse rates

One newly qualified teacher used a spreadsheet to support science teaching – children aged nine and ten years recorded their pulse rates during a whole-class lesson and then small groups transferred data to the spreadsheet. In each group, one child typed in the data, while the others watched and then recorded the data into their own science books. The disadvantage of this is that although they all see a spreadsheet being used, some have little experience of using the tool themselves. Another scientific use of ICT was with a Dorling Kindersley encyclopaedia on CD-ROM. Children had access to this through the school network, so they did not need to load the CD-ROM onto individual machines. They particularly focused on video clips of the human body, muscle movements and heart pumping blood. Children then wrote an explanation of how muscles work and drew pictures in their own science books.

## Animals and sounds

A student teacher working in a Year 1 class (children aged five and six years) used another Dorling Kindersley CD-ROM resource that contained pictures of animals and the sounds they make. Because this was a noisy activity, the teacher provided head-phones for those children who worked inside the classroom. Others working in an alcove nearby with the student teacher and the laptops just managed without the headphones. The student's lesson plan identified science as the main subject, linked to a QCA unit on sound and hearing, with a cross-curricular link to ICT and to literacy skills:

> 'Children in purple and orange groups used *My First Amazing Dictionary* to match sounds with pictures of objects in a game-type activity, also involved vocabulary.'

## Plants and ICT tools

In a Year 3/4 class (ages from seven to nine years), the student teacher used a digital camera in one science activity about the growth of plants. She also used a website called 'Espresso' (http://www.espresso.co.uk/) for a plant growth video clip to show the children simulations of how plants grow. The children used 'Notepad' (a simple word processor) to record their ideas. Having taught the children how to use Notepad and the Internet as a whole class, the student benefited from the use of the learning assistant to support a group of children who were working in pairs to get information from the website. The student had already set up the PCs to access this site and prepared the question 'What can you find out about plants?' using Word herself to prepare this open-ended worksheet. She used six computers in that lesson – three PCs and three laptops. The children also used a paint program to draw plants and plant-related pictures.

## Summary

In this chapter, you have seen examples of the work of student and newly qualified teachers using ICT in four different settings; one student used a digital camera, website and an interactive whiteboard to teach about light and shadows; another used a computer suite to explore the Internet; the third example was of the use of ICT in a biological exploration of the school grounds; and the final case study explored how a school uses laptops to support science. You should now be able to:

- Analyse setting, context and environment in your own experience and use these ideas to help you organise your teaching more effectively.

- Recognise the advantages and limitations of computer suites for teaching science.

- Plan a lesson on science in the school grounds, where digital equipment supports the science learning objectives.

- Recognise the reasons for using laptops within the classroom during lessons with cross-curricular links.

## Web links

www.ase.org.uk
The Association of Science Education.

www.ngfl.gov.uk
The National Grid for Learning.

http://www.planet-science.com/home.html
Planet science website does have some fun stuff.

www.espresso.co.uk
A commercial site for resources for teaching.

http://vtc.ngfl.gov.uk/vtc
Virtual Teachers' Centre containing useful ideas for teaching.

http://www.Scl-Journal.org/
The Science Journal site shows work done by school and college students.

www.ex.ac.uk/Mirrors/nineplanets
This site at Exeter University is typical of many that deal with space and the solar system.

http://library.advanced.org/11924
This US site has a lot of interesting background knowledge about science and scientists.

www.ask.co.uk
A useful and easy-to-use search engine is Ask Jeeves.

http://www.ajkids.com/
This children's version of Ask Jeeves may give better results.

http://www.sparkisland.com
A commercial site with many science resources.

www.yahooligans.com
A US children's search engine.

http://www.oxfam.org.uk/coolplanet
An interesting site from Oxfam.

http://www.wwtlearn.org.uk/index0.html
The Wild Fowl and Wetlands Trust.

http://www.bbc.co.uk/learning/
British Broadcasting Corporation learning site.

http://www.bbc.co.uk/schools/podsmission/
BBC again for some science about bones, electricity or solids and liquids.

http://www.bbc.co.uk/schools/revisewise/science/living/ 04_act.shtml
Tests, worksheets and activities on science.

http://www.channel4.com/science/index.html
'Ask an Expert' section and a life stories section to help with information about famous scientists.

http://www.channel4.com/learning/primary.html
Lesson plans.

http://www.4learning.co.uk/apps/homework/index.jsp
A homework site.

# Flight

## Introduction

This chapter explores a variety of activities and ideas about forces, in the context of flight or movement through the air. It looks at flight as a human activity, as well as flying objects from the natural world, and suggests ways of helping children understand some of the forces that make flight possible. A series of questions is explored, as well as some of the common misconceptions children experience and ways to help them replace these with more scientific ideas and concepts. The use of ICT comes from a number of areas, including data handling, communication and sources of information.

## Learning objectives

By the end of the chapter, you should be able to:

- Recognise a number of activities suitable for carrying out in the classroom to support children's understanding of movements through the air.

- Identify children's common misconceptions about movement through the air and be able to plan lessons to address these ideas.

- Help children to use ICT tools and skills to enable them to perceive and present patterns in data.

- Help children to use spreadsheets to predict relationships in scientific data gathered during investigations of the fall of parachutes.

**TABLE 4.1  ICT National Curriculum links**

|  | Key Stage 1 (ages 5–7) | Key Stage 2 (ages 8–11) |
|---|---|---|
| Birds and feathers | 1a, 2c, 2d, 3b, 5b | 1a, 1b, 5a |
| Spinners and fair testing | 1a, 3a | 1c, 2a, 4a |
| Parachutes, variables and air resistance | 1a, 3a | 1b, 2c, 5a, 5b |

**TABLE 4.2  QCA scheme links**

|  | Science | ICT |
|---|---|---|
| Birds and feathers | 1E | 1B |
| Spinners and fair testing | 2E | 3C |
| Parachutes, variables and air resistance | 4E, 6E | 6A, 6D |

For example, in the Year 4 unit for science (4E Friction), children should be introduced to movement through water, so that they are experiencing friction in a different form from the force between two solid objects. One of the suggested activities for children – running while holding a large sheet of card in this unit – is intended to lead them to considering air resistance as a frictional force, which is necessary for them to begin to understand the forces acting on flying objects. Another activity is making and testing parachutes, as a way to relate this to their understanding of air resistance. The falling of pieces of paper is suggested as an activity in Unit 6E, followed up with suggestions about making and testing spinners.

Looking at the QCA scheme for ICT, you can find several examples of the ways in which flight can provide a context for learning and developing ICT skills. For example, in 1B Using a word bank, children need to gather information from a variety of sources such as people, books, databases, CD-ROMs, videos and TV; while in Unit 3C Introduction to databases, they could be making their own database from data about parachutes or spinners. Also in this chapter, spreadsheets are used for presenting and manipulating data from experiments, helping children to predict and then check their predictions.

## Flight as a big idea

Force is seen as one of the five big ideas in the revision of the Key Stage 3 Science National Curriculum. The document (DfES 2002: 18) does not say why it is a big idea, just that:

Pupils need to extend their thinking from concrete examples of forces to a more abstract view, for example, they need to understand that the state of motion of a body depends on the sum of the forces acting upon it.

This idea is relatively easy to introduce with flight, since children can experience the various forces separately and then explore them through investigations and ICT. These forces include gravity and air resistance (or drag), although this chapter does not deal with lift forces, as the Bernoulli effect is too complex for children in the 5–11 age range.

## 4.1 Birds and feathers

A wider look (i.e. the perspectives from a number of subjects, including art, design, maths, RE, history) at flight could be the context for a number of more specific science and ICT activities. The symbolism of flight in religion and cultures could be a focus for our understanding of the significance of flight in the human experience. Can you think of examples from different places and settings, for example, the image of the dove carrying a twig in its mouth in the biblical story of Noah and the Flood? Are there further examples which come from non-Christian religions and belief systems? Historical themes and topics as well as religious and cultural ones can be linked to scientific ideas, as long as there are specific scientific learning objectives. An interesting story to start an investigation is that of Icarus and Daedalus, originating in Ancient Greek mythology. This father and son team of ancient Greeks made wings, holding the feathers together with wax. In the story, the wings are powerful enough to carry the weight of a man high into the air, so high that he gets close to the sun and the wax melts. This makes the feathers come loose and the wings disintegrate, plunging the flier to his doom. But would the wings really have got hotter as Icarus flew higher in the sky? In fact, as you rise through the atmosphere, the air gets colder, not hotter.

### Art, science and ICT – using search engines

Another interesting cross-curricular link could come through the connection between science, ICT and art, through the context of birds. Although many birds have fascinating colours and shapes, and their feathers have been a traditional source of inspiration for children making close observational drawings and paintings, there is also potential for birds to be used as a starting point for science and ICT explorations.

There are several commercial and charitable websites that provide pictures and information about birds, and some primary schools have put information on their own websites about their work about birds.

### Search engines

Two relatively simple search engines, Google (www.google.co.uk) and Ask Jeeves (www.ask.co.uk) would produce appropriate results about birds and feathers. A quick search of Ask Jeeves for the terms 'primary education birds' produced several appropriate websites, which would be relevant for children, although searching for the term 'find feathers' was much less useful, as it gave information at too complex a level. Google searches for the words 'feathers birds' also produced websites that were relevant and interesting, with some detailed pictures of feathers, but with text that children might find difficult to read and understand.

## Feathers as a starting point

Feathers themselves are another good starting point, partly because you can find them just lying around in a park and partly since they perform some interesting movements in the air if you drop them from about two metres up. Some flight feathers will spin as they drop, but often in a very jerky movement. Others will float gently down, but may sway from side to side as they fall. Others may just drop straight down. Children should be encouraged to suggest some possible explanations for these differences and then to test them. (It is necessary to take care with using materials like feathers picked up in the open, as they may contain harmful bacteria and micro-organisms – it is important to disinfect these before using them with children.)

## Children's explanations

Here are two examples of explanations that children make:

*Child 1:* Maybe it's because the feather is thicker on one side that makes it fall kind of sideways?

*Child 2:* I think the feathers with both sides equal will just fall straight down, because the air pushes them back evenly on both sides.

The Nuffield-Collins teachers' books based on the SPACE (1995) project are a useful source of ideas and information on ways of following up children's ideas and turning them into investigations.

## Observation and comparison

So after these first exploratory observations and tentative explanations, provide children with more (cleaned and disinfected) feathers with similar features and ask them to observe them, to look for similarities and differences in the way they fall (Science National Curriculum, DfEE 1999). One way to motivate children in this kind of observation activity is to ask them to compete for which groups can find the most similarities or the most differences.

## Researching birds and flight

This could also lead to further exploration of the structure and functions of feathers through books, CD-ROMs and the Internet. In order to maintain motivation and to adopt a creative approach to both science and ICT, at this stage of the work a teacher should encourage children to follow up their own interests or to explore the lifestyles of birds in different environments. Teachers should suggest, rather than direct children, for example to explore the history of birds from prehistoric times, through exploring a simulation like a virtual museum. A creative teacher would provide the resources and time for children to explore the history of human flight, including the designs for flying machines by Leonardo da Vinci, some of which were based on the structure of bats' wings, others based on rotating blades similar to helicopters.

## Making and testing models

An extension to this would be to design and make some model feathers, using materials like paper and plastics, and test these models by dropping them and comparing the way they fall with real feathers. This would involve looking for patterns with the help of ICT tools. A fun model can be made by inserting the shafts of five or six feathers into a large cork, rather like a shuttlecock, and testing how well it flies through the air.

## Digital photos

Video and still digital cameras can help children to record, analyse and present ideas about the more difficult movements of birds and even of the larger flying insects. Most primary schools in the UK now have digital cameras and the relevant software to turn the images into both electronic and print versions. This would link to the QCA ICT Unit 6A on Making multimedia presentations.

## Using questioning

In section 12.1 of Chapter 12, we look at some general types of questions which a teacher might ask to help children focus on specific concepts and to explore alternative ideas. Of course, it is also important to set up situations in which children themselves raise questions and then try to answer these questions by investigating in practical ways.

When you are preparing lessons, it can be helpful to jot down some questions to keep the discussion focused on your main learning objectives. The SPACE project followed up its research with teachers' guides that show a number of useful questions and some of the possible answers that children might give, followed by some suggestions for activities.

## 4.2 Spinners and fair testing

In the context of flight, here are a few ideas for questioning children. The context for these questions is that children have been looking at feathers and found that some of them spin in the air as they drop. They also have a collection of sycamore or maple tree seeds and other seeds from trees that move or spin as they fall through the air.

'What do you think will happen if we let it drop from here?' (indicating a higher or lower starting point for the drop)

'What do you think makes it go round rather than falling straight down?'

'What did you notice that's the same about these two?' (for example, seeds from a sycamore or maple tree)

'What did you notice that's different about them?'

'What can we measure about them?'

It can be useful to divide questions up into those that start up scientific thinking and those that support further ideas about the topic or possible answers to questions.

'What did you notice that's different about them?'

This question often works well in the flight context, for example, in comparing the appearance and flight patterns of birds. Looking at feathers can also provide children with some clues about the ways in which birds behave in flight.

'What do you think caused it to happen?' Put this into the context of replying to an observation the child has reported, such as 'it spins round' after watching a seed dropping.

'What did it remind you of?'

This is a useful question if we want children to relate the science in school with their experiences in everyday life (see Chapters 7 and 11 for further examples of teaching and learning from everyday experiences and from visits out of school).

'Why do you think that?'

This should give rise to children explaining the reasoning behind their ideas. We might help them by suggesting some of the possible sources of their thinking, for example, 'someone told me', like a bigger sister or brother, a parent or carer, or teacher. It could be that children get some of their science ideas from TV documentaries like nature programmes or films like *Star Wars*. You could easily ask the whole class if their ideas came from books, through a show of hands. What other sources of information and ideas do you think might be forthcoming from your class? Interactive whiteboards provide an easy way of saving these ideas and making them available for future lessons.

## A few common misconceptions and how to deal with them

### Heavier things fall faster than lighter ones

There are probably some areas where we do not know the source of our thinking. Many adults think that a heavier object drops faster than a lighter one. The best way of dealing with this misconception is to examine a couple of film containers, one with a lump of plasticine or clay inside it, the other empty. It may seem so obvious that no explanation has ever been thought necessary. But this demonstration (try it out on a friend) does at least make you ask questions, even if the scientific explanation that involves the concept of momentum may be too abstract for some children.

There is no gravity on the moon, because there is no atmosphere

It is true that there is no atmosphere on the moon. Any gases that ever existed on the moon have been lost into space as gravity on the moon is much less than that on the earth (about one-tenth of earth gravity). But the moon still does have enough gravity to keep a layer of dust on much of its surface, and for spacemen to have walked on the surface even though they bounced high as they did so. You might be able to deal with this misconception by showing a clip of a video of spacemen walking on the moon and asking children to discuss it. Another way might be to raise the issue of why there are tides in the oceans on the earth – a result of the moon's gravitational influence on the earth.

Parachutes work best with light weights

Although parachutes do fall at slower speeds with lighter weights, there is a limit to the best ratio of weight to canopy areas. Making parachute models and testing them for their stability as well as their rate of fall can deal with this idea. Children will find that with very small weights, the parachutes may turn over in the air or are so unstable that they do not fall regularly but waft around in the air like some feathers do.

Seeds spin because the way gravity works in the northern hemisphere is different from in the south, like water going down a plughole in opposite directions in north or south

Contacting classes in different countries and asking them to co-operate on experiments related to gravity would be a perfect way to integrate ICT, science and English writing and reading skills with real audiences. Children in New Zealand or Australia would be in a good position to contrast with children in the UK or North America. Schools could put their results on their own websites and invite others to look at them and then provide further ideas or questions.

## Misconceptions tables

In subsequent chapters, tables with a common format will be used to describe common misconceptions and ways in which they might be addressed.

**TABLE 4.3** Misconceptions about flight

| |
|---|
| **Common misconception** There is no gravity on the moon, because there is no atmosphere. |
| **Usual age for misconception** All ages, including some adults. |
| **The scientific explanation** The moon has mass, so it must also have gravity, but its mass is less than that of the earth, so its gravitational attraction is less. Any gases there once were in the moon's atmosphere have been lost. |
| **Ways to address the misconception** Discussion of tides and the influence of the moon's gravity on the earth – showing video of spacemen walking on the moon. |

## 4.3 Parachutes, variables and air resistance

Another example of a creative approach to the theme of flight is an investigation into the behaviour of parachutes, which deals with maths and data handling as well as science and ICT. The QCA scheme Unit 4E Friction mentions air resistance as a force that slows objects moving through air. Then it suggests an activity making parachutes and raising questions like 'Does the size of the parachute affect how long it takes to fall?'

The QCA unit suggests, as a starting point, a discussion about windy days and riding a bicycle, and links to previous activities within the unit about movement through water. Starting points for a series of lessons on parachutes would be looking at things in the environment, which float or are easily blown around on a windy day. A brainstorm with the whole class should allow you to identify many of the variables that can be investigated. But before children can realistically do this, they will need to 'play' or explore some model parachutes first. This part of the scheme could be carried out with a small group of children or you could do a similar exercise as was suggested with the spinners activity earlier in the chapter. Each child or pair of children could make a small model parachute to a simple pattern provided by the teacher, perhaps linked to design and technology curriculum requirements. They could then suggest alterations to the basic design in order to improve the performance of their model and at this stage the brainstorm could take place. You would need to decide how to proceed, depending on the time available to you.

## Databases and variables with parachutes

If you want to save the data from a number of children about their parachute models, you need to help them set up some common factors, as well as identifying the particular factor or variable they have chosen to investigate. Each variable could then be used as a separate field in a database you set up to record and present the results of the investigation.

Variable 1: the canopy, its size, material, shape. This variable could be split into three fields in a database.

Variable 2: the weight of the load, including strings, if appropriate.

Variable 3: the strings, their length and number. Again, these could be three separate fields in a database.

Variable 4: the height of the drop.

Result 1: Time taken to reach floor.

Result 2: Displacement from vertical.

## Measuring time

When children are too young for sophisticated time measurement, they can think about and decide upon non-standard measurements, for example, by counting quickly and evenly. Although each child might get a different number, they could still compare the patterns in their own data, as long as they each counted at the same rate each time. This would work well with children in the early years or Key Stage 1.

For older and more skilled children, this could lead to an interesting way to personalise the experiment, as well as an opportunity to see which method (personal counting or stopwatches) gave the better pattern or conformed better to the predicted outcomes. For example, predict that doubling the drop will less than double the time, because gravity produces an acceleration, not just a constant speed, so the longer the drop the relatively shorter the time. Half the class could use stopwatches, the other half personal counting. Digital stopwatches are better for some children because they provide a clearer reading, in numbers rather than through the hands of a clock face.

## An extension activity for older or more experienced children

Returning to the original problem about whether a parachute travels faster at the start of its fall or towards the end, an alternative hypothesis is that the parachute falls fast right at the start, before it traps enough air. But from then on, it falls at a constant speed and does not accelerate – this is the balance point between the gravity force and the air resistance force. So the longer it falls, the relatively more slowly it is going, compared to the start. Any of these hypotheses can be tested by plotting the various factors against time and by using the data to predict numerically.

## Spreadsheets for data

Table 4.4 is an Excel spreadsheet with data, sorted in the time category in descending order. From this you can see a rough correlation with the weight of the parachute, although it is not exact as there are other variables affecting the outcomes. Data of this type may be too complex for children in Year 4 classes, but would be possible with older or more experienced children.

It links to National Curriculum ICT section 2C:

Developing ideas and making things happen – to use simulations and explore models in order to answer 'What if …' questions, to investigate and evaluate the effect of changing values and to identify patterns and relationships [for example, simulation software, spreadsheet models].
(DfEE 1999: 100)

The data could then be explored further in order to predict the outcome of a new set of experiments with only one parameter changed for each parachute. In this case, we might choose height as the changed parameter, predicting that doubling the height would double the time taken to fall to the ground. Now the spreadsheet can be edited

**TABLE 4.4** Parachute investigations

| Canopy size in sq. cm. | Canopy shape | Canopy material | String length in cm. | String type | Height of drop in m. | Weight in g. | Displacement in cm. | Time of fall in secs |
|---|---|---|---|---|---|---|---|---|
| 40 | square | silk | 30 | cotton | 2 | 50 | 1.3 | 2.3 |
| 45 | square | silk | 20 | plastic | 2 | 50 | 3.6 | 2.4 |
| 35 | square | silk | 24 | cotton | 2 | 30 | 4 | 2.6 |
| 40 | square | silk | 30 | plastic | 2 | 35 | 2.2 | 3 |
| 40 | square | silk | 20 | plastic | 2 | 30 | 2.5 | 3.2 |
| 50 | rectang | cotton | 30 | cotton | 2 | 40 | 4.7 | 3.5 |
| 55 | rectang | cotton | 20 | cotton | 2 | 40 | 5.1 | 3.9 |
| 40 | rectang | cotton | 25 | plastic | 2 | 30 | 4.5 | 4.5 |
| 50 | rectang | cotton | 25 | plastic | 2 | 30 | 4.2 | 4.8 |

so that only certain cells are highlighted – those that are relevant to the specific prediction being made. Table 4.5 shows the two sets of cells concerning time of fall, the first being the actual measurements made and the second is the predicted outcome after doubling the distance of the drop (see Frost 2002: 106 for examples of spreadsheets and parachutes).

**TABLE 4.5** Part of an Excel spreadsheet on parachute data

| Time of fall 1 in sec. | Time of fall 2 in secs |
|---|---|
| 2.3 | 4.6 |
| 2.4 | 4.8 |
| 2.6 | 5.2 |
| 3 | 6 |
| 3.2 | 6.4 |
| 3.5 | 7 |
| 3.9 | 7.8 |
| 4.5 | 9 |
| 4.8 | 9.6 |

**TABLE 4.6** A simplified medium-term plan for parachute theme

| Preparation by teacher | Week 1 | Week 2 | Week 3 | Week 4 |
|---|---|---|---|---|
| Collect resources. | Dropping things, like seeds and papers. | Pairs make alternative model. | In ICT suite, whole class decides on Excel spreadsheet details. | In classroom, spreadsheet used to present and review data. |
| Prepare learning outcomes. | Make simple parachute models. | Groups of four plan and test new models. | Pairs of children enter their own data on spreadsheet. | Spreadsheet used for prediction. |
| Start constructing lesson plans. | Plan and carry out a test of the simple models. | Groups of four make records of models and results on paper. | Whole class combines data in class record. | Testing prediction with new investigation. |
| Organise other adults to help. | | | | |
| Find and book suite to carry out investigations and computer activities. | Pairs of children plan the construction of alternative model. | | | Interpreting results and preparing class assembly on the scheme. |

As the work with parachutes would be likely to need more than a single lesson, Table 4.6 contains some thoughts about how a medium-term plan could be constructed. How does a scheme of work differ from a lesson plan?

## Schemes of work

The scheme must fit in with previous teaching and learning, so you need to find out what children have done before. In a settled school or class, where most children have been in the school continuously, this is less of a problem, as you can ask the previous teacher, look up saved schemes or refer to the school's long-term plans. But this task is more difficult in schools or classes where there has been a high turnover of teachers. This situation can often arise in inner city areas, where staff changes occur every year or even several times in a year, or where a stream of supply teachers has been employed to cover staff absences or shortages. Some schools also experience rapid changes in the pupil population, due to housing, local employment, migration or other causes. In these volatile situations, your best solution is to stick closely to national guidelines, such as the QCA schemes and National Curriculum documents.

The sorts of resources likely to be needed include:

- For the parachute canopies – plastic bags, bin liners, thin fabrics like synthetic materials and cotton or specialised kite-making fabrics.

- String, thread, embroidery cotton or other non-tangling materials. (Plasticated string is usually useless.)

- Scissors, hole-punchers, rulers, circular objects (to draw round), other templates (to ensure standard canopy sizes).

- Loads of various types that can be attached easily – metal washers are a good choice, or small weights that can be tied on, or polystyrene cups that can carry a variety of changing loads and are easy to attach to the strings; plasticene or modelling clay (as some children like to make realistic figures to be carried on their model parachutes).

- Weighing scales are also useful, but should be carefully chosen so that children can use them easily and so that they are accurate enough to record the small differences likely to be encountered. Newton meters (commonly known as spring balances) are ideal in this investigation as long as they are sensitive to about 10 grams.

**TABLE 4.7** Possible recording frame for pair parachute model

| Names of children (Afia and Tommy) | Data |
| --- | --- |
| Canopy shape | Hexagon |
| Canopy size | 40 sq. cm. |
| Canopy material | Black bin liner |
| Number of strings | Six |
| Type of strings | Etc… |
| Load weight | Etc… |
| Type of load | |
| Height of drop | |
| Displacement from vertical | |
| Stability | |
| Etc… | |
| Etc… | |

## Recording the results

To help children record their results, you might consider using simple recording grids. Table 4.7 shows a writing/recording frame to help a pair of children to record the details of their own model. The details of the data to be entered should depend on the results of the children's ideas about what they think is important information, collected from a brainstorm. You could develop a further table to support group recording or whole-class records.

## Summary

In this chapter, you have seen how the theme of flight can be explored in creative ways, how spreadsheets and databases can be used for handling data and supporting scientific predictions, and how the Internet and interactive whiteboards can help teachers to present information and ideas to children.

You should now be able to:

- Recognise a number of starting points for science investigations about the forces involved in the movement of objects through the air.
- Identify some of the more common misconceptions about forces.
- Plan lessons, using ICT, to help children overcome some of these misconceptions.
- Use ICT tools to help children perceive patterns and data and test out their predictions.

## Web links

www.nc.uk.net
This is the National Curriculum online version.

http://www.ajkids.com/
This is the children's version of Ask Jeeves.

http://www.gwydir.demon.co.uk/jo/myths.htm
A children's site for myths and legends.

www.google.co.uk
A search engine.

## CHAPTER

# 5

# Sustainability and living things

## Introduction

The aim of the chapter is to show how the techniques of science and the tools provided by ICT can help children learn about the 'big idea' of sustainability. You might wish to link this big idea with parts of other chapters (e.g. 'Food and energy' and the concept of 'alive' in sections 8.3 and 8.4 in Chapter 8). 'Education for sustainability' can cut across all subjects and links with the rationale of why we educate children. The reasons for teaching and the ways in which we teach are connected by the theories that we use to justify our teaching methods. Sustainability itself is a complex concept and the introduction to this chapter attempts to show how it can be analysed in the context of the education of teachers.

## Learning objectives

By the end of this chapter you should be able to plan and teach aspects of:

- Ourselves, similarities and differences, and our place within the world using databases, email and the Internet, digital cameras, CD-ROMs and data logging.

- Ethics and living things through investigations with minibeasts, using ICT tools such as digital microscopes and sensors, CD-ROMs, the Internet and interactive whiteboards.

- Environment and habitats, by investigating and observing animals and plants – leading to the concept of diversity, using design programs like Kid Pix, clip art and email.

**TABLE 5.1    ICT National Curriculum links**

|  | Key Stage 1 (ages 5–7) | Key Stage 2 (ages 8–11) |
|---|---|---|
| Ourselves as humans | 1a, 2a, 3a, 5b | 1a, 1b, 3a |
| Investigating animals | 1a, 5b | 2b, 5a |
| Environments and habitats | 1a, 2a, 3b | 1b, 3a, 5a, 5b |

**TABLE 5.2   QCA scheme links**

|  | Science | ICT |
|---|---|---|
| Ourselves as humans | 1A, 2A, 3A, 4A, 5A | 3C, 4C, 5B, 5D |
| Investigating animals | 2B, 4A, 5B, 6A | 2B, 2E, 6D |
| Environments and habitats | 1B, 2B, 2C, 3B, 4B, 5B, 5/6H | 3A, 3E, 4A |

## Why is sustainability a big idea?

### Environmental education

The concept of sustainability has its roots in environmental education and in personal and social education and citizenship. Environmental education has more obvious curriculum links with science (and geography). It is often split into three aspects – education:

■ about the environment

■ through and in the environment

■ for the environment

Learning about the environment suggests that children should study things and events within an environmental framework, such as animals and plants in a natural environment or humans in a built environment. Learning through the environment means that we use environmental contexts to teach scientific concepts or mathematical skills or poetry. Learning for the environment implies a values approach to the world around us, caring for it, preserving the 'better' parts of it and taking action to prevent the destruction of parts of it. It is perhaps this third aspect of environmental education that leads to the big idea of sustainability and education for sustainability.

### Sustainability in teacher education

Sustainability ideas have been analysed for teacher education by Griffen *et al.* (2002) into sections about knowledge and understanding, skills, values and dispositions. The idea of dispositions comes from the concept of action competence. Jensen and Schnack (1994) suggest, 'a school does not become green by conserving energy, collecting batteries or sorting waste. The crucial factor must be what the pupils learn from participating in such activities – or helping to decide something else' (pp. 6–7).

One problem for teachers is how far to go in transferring these ideas to children of different ages and in school contexts that are not necessarily in agreement with some of these. Encouraging 'empathy with others' would be a worthwhile objective for both teachers and children, but would 'democratic leadership' be a useful skill for a primary

**TABLE 5.3** Sustainability issues in teacher education

| Sustainability ideas analysed | Personal value | Teaching importance |
|---|---|---|
| **Knowledge and understanding** of sustainability required of new teachers can be broken down into:<br>■ Relation of people to the physical environment<br>■ Understanding of finite resources<br>■ Understanding of potential for change<br>■ Possible and preferable futures<br>■ Lifestyles for a more sustainable world | | |
| **Skills** can also be broken down into:<br>■ Listening to others and valuing their contributions<br>■ Collaboration<br>■ Empathy<br>■ Handling and resolving conflict<br>■ Making informed decisions<br>■ Building pupils' self-esteem<br>■ Sustaining effective discussion and argument<br>■ Ability to critically analyse<br>■ Ability to detect and challenge bias and stereotype<br>■ Risk taking<br>■ Leading through distributed or democratic leadership | | |
| Finally the **values and dispositions** needed are:<br>■ Valuing the physical environment<br>■ Valuing and celebrating diversity *(Diversity is also a science concept related to evolution – hence a big idea in itself)*<br>■ Commitment to justice and equality<br>■ Empathy with others<br>■ Respect and caring for ourselves and others including future generations<br>■ Openness and commitment to lifelong learning<br>■ Commitment to a lifestyle consistent with sustainable development | | |

school pupil to develop? It would be an interesting exercise to look at them in terms of your own attitudes to teaching across the curriculum in a primary school and see how far you would agree with them or think of them as priorities. How far would you, as a student or newly qualified teacher, value 'risk taking' in a science or ICT lesson? Would you think that 'building pupils' self-esteem' would be a useful learning objective from a lesson that used ICT to support science teaching and learning?

**Directed Activity 5.1    Exploring your own attitudes to sustainability**

**Age range**
Your own age.

**Size of group**
One, or more if you can find others of your own age to discuss this with.

**Specific questions raised**
How do you feel about sustainability?
How do you think your own values and beliefs should affect the ways in which you teach?

**Background to the activity**
Read through the list of knowledge and understanding, skills, values and dispositions above.

**The activity**
Photocopy Table 5.3.
Assign each phrase a numerical value indicating its importance to you personally, from 1 (most important) to 3 (least important).
Then, beside that grading, indicate, using the same scale, how important you think the items would be when teaching children in the primary school.
See if you can find a colleague to do the same exercise and discuss the differences and similarities in your scoring of the issues. If there are differences, why do you think they exist?

## 5.1 Ourselves as humans

### Compare yourself to another animal

Very young children, once they start to observe and talk about what they see, are already beginning to compare themselves to other animals:

> *Child Cha. (age 2 years)*: 'I've got eyes, cat's got eyes, dog licks me, dog has a tongue like me, like Daddy, like Mummy.'

Children are starting to make sense of the world and beginning to use conceptual frameworks, which we would classify as early science process skills. Such development can be supported through providing further real examples of animals, but also through ICT tools, such as *My World 3 Body and Face* (Research Machines software). These pieces of software encourage children to compare their own bodies and faces with those of another child and to label the body and face parts. The use of speech in the software helps children with special needs (who may be unable to read fluently) or pupils who need support with the English language because they are learning English as an Additional Language (EAL) to recognise parts of the human body: 'Pupils should be taught to recognize and compare the main external parts of the bodies of humans and other animals' (National Curriculum Science DfEE 1999: 79).

## Online interactive whiteboard lessons

Online lesson plans are available from a number of websites to support science teaching and learning, but should always be adapted to the needs of your own class. One of the more recent developments in ICT hardware in primary schools is the provision of interactive whiteboards in normal classrooms (as well as in computer rooms). Lesson plans for use with these boards can be downloaded from the Internet, for example, from a Canadian Smart Board company (http://edcompass.smarttech.com/en/learning/activities/notebook.aspx). One plan about nutrition, which has some connection with sustainability education (making informed decisions), is aimed at 10- to 12-year-olds and it links with other websites (www.sciencenetlinks.com and http://exhibits.pacsci.org/nutrition/sleuth/sleuth.html). The lesson plan aims to show children what proper nutrition is and asks them to look at their own diet to see if it is balanced. It goes on to discuss the roles of calcium and several vitamins in diet, asks children to interact by listing the foods they have eaten and compare them to a food pyramid diagram. There will be more online resources like this becoming available to support the use of interactive whiteboards, as these items become more widespread in primary schools across the world. Try an Internet search of UK and USA sites that provide lessons, but be wary of just applying them to your own situation without some adaptation to the needs of your own curriculum and the learning objectives that are suited to the children in your class or group.

## What sort of food do people need?

Ourselves and our need for food is another useful starting point for both science and ICT and links to the knowledge and understanding aspects of sustainability – 'relation of people to the physical environment' and 'lifestyles for a more sustainable world'. ICT tools that can be useful include software that looks at healthy eating and exercise. A good source for evaluating software is Schoolzone (http://www.schoolzone.co.uk/evaluations/findeval.htm). Software like 'It's your goal' (http://www.itsyourgoal.com/) can help children to explore the effects of diet and healthy eating on the ability to perform tasks and activities like playing football. One of the major concerns of health educators in the developed world is the sedentary lifestyle of many young people. (It is, however, debatable whether interacting with a computer and software is more healthy that actually playing a game of football.)

## Grow your own food

See Chapter 8 on energy for further work on this idea. A link to the idea of growing food plants is to carry out surveys with children about their personal lifestyles, comparing their own eating habits with those of others in different countries. Email could be used to do this sort of work. Although it might seem attractive to link up your own class with another in a developing country, there are often problems about this because of the different emphasis on children having access to computers and the Internet. So it might be easier to carry out this kind of email link with a school in the USA, Canada, Australia or New Zealand, where the majority language is English and the ICT environments may be more similar. One also needs to explore stereotypical reactions among children and try to find ways to dispel these views. It can be interesting to compare children's favourite foods with their views on what constitutes healthy eating and then challenge them about the discrepancies.

## Focus on your hands

One starting point for getting children to think about ourselves as part of the natural world, rather than just as people who are different from all other natural living things, is to compare us to other animals. A focus on one part of us is usually better with younger children, for example, our eyes, as in Chapter 6 on light and colour.

Another interesting focus could be on our hands, which are often very different from the front limbs of most mammals but are similar to some. Ask the children to collect pictures of animals and compare their limbs, and the equivalent of front paws, hands, hooves or wings. Can they recognise reasons for these differences and similarities in terms of hunters and hunted animals, or carnivores that use sight to help them catch prey versus those that use their limbs in other ways? What significance is there in these differences? (For older children, what about the ethics of using animals like horses and dogs to race for our own enjoyment?) Children can use a variety of sources to explore these questions about animal form and function. Look up the BECTa website for resources on CD-ROM or other software (http://besd.becta.org.uk/). Help them to search the Internet for information about animals and their environments.

## The bones project

An interesting, long-term project, which has been reported extensively elsewhere (Mitra in Leask and Meadows 2000), is one about bones. This project helped children aged between seven and nine years to look at how people break their bones; the children used multimedia authoring to present results. Children used a variety of practical science, information seeking and ICT tools in this project as well as inviting outside experts to help them learn about bones. They conducted surveys and used word processors to complete the survey sheets; used scanners to duplicate copies of their drawings of animal bones; learnt how to use digital cameras and tape recorders to make records of information gathered from books and from experts.

## A bags project

People in the modern world use much more technology in their everyday lives, some of which has an impact on the environment (linking to the disposition about commitment to a lifestyle consistent with sustainable development). When we go shopping for our food, we use bags to carry it. Ask children to collect a range of types of bags that are used for this purpose and examine their properties critically. Or take a look at the bags they use to carry things to school and back again. Are they reusable – does your school supply special bags or do your parents give you bags that are stronger than plastic, throwaway bags? Can you use the Internet to make a survey of bags throughout history or containers generally and identify the science behind, for example, bags for carrying tools or containers that hold liquids? What are the advantages and disadvantages of different types of container? Can you design a bag that would be good for carrying your wet swimming things back from the pool or the beach, but which would also be environmentally friendlier than a plastic bag?

## 5.2 Investigating animals

### Controversial issues

There are controversial issues that need to be dealt with when you start to investigate living things, especially living animals, in primary schools. Big ideas in everyday life include whether to use animals to test medicines, whether animals should be kept in cages in zoos or whether it is right to eat meat. In schools, children can start to think about even quite complex issues, if we focus the ideas on things and events that interest them and where they have some experience. A class of five-year-olds will be able to recognise a picture of a polar bear on an ice floe and suggest consequences of warming on the situation, as long as they know that ice melts when it gets warmer. This could lead them to investigate how fast ice melts, using ice cubes wrapped in a variety of materials, like cotton wool, cooking foil or paper. A more appropriate discussion and possible investigation for eight- or nine-year-olds might be about whether we should keep animals like rabbits in school. A role-play discussion could be set up so that children could act as the rabbits, giving their opinions, as well as the potential predators of rabbits in the wild, or the opinions of a child who likes to care for and stroke the rabbit. A consequence chart might be a suitable way of organising the recording of such a discussion or role play (Ratcliffe and Lock 1998: 85–87).

### Saving children's ideas for future reference

Fair testing and a range of variables would need to be considered by the children. This consequence chart would be drawn using a variety of ICT tools, such as tables, text boxes or PowerPoint slides. But it seems particularly suited to use with Smart software on an interactive whiteboard, so that children's ideas could be entered by them and the whole map saved for future use in other lessons. An alternative would be for children to save their ideas in their own section of the school network, using a normal word processor or a word bank. *My World 3* or *Clicker 3* software (available from Research

**TABLE 5.4** Consequence chart – animals in schools

| Stimulus and sequence | Questions, answers and choices |
|---|---|
| Starting question: | 'Should animals be kept in schools?' |
| Leads to possible answers: | **1** Yes, so that we can look after them.<br>**2** No, because they should be free to roam in the wild. |
| This could lead to further questions: | **1** How should we look after them?<br>**2** What happens to wild rabbits – what tries to eat them?<br>**3** What do rabbits like to eat? |
| This leads to investigations, with a choice of variables: | **1** Choices of foods<br>**2** Number of rabbits<br>**3** Times of the day |

Machines and other companies) would support the needs of children who find writing difficult.

## 'What if' questions

'What if' questions (see Chapter 9, 'What if a chair was made of chocolate?') are another form of inquiry, with relevance for science and ICT, which can lead to investigations with living things, for example, 'What if we let the rabbits out into the school garden, instead of keeping them in hutches in the hall?' Some of the aims of this sort of activity are:

- encouraging a respect for evidence
- open-mindedness
- the ability to tolerate uncertainty
- the opportunity to make up your own mind
- the chance to develop your own opinions

## Investigations

Chapter 1 introduced the five different types of investigations that Harlen (2000: 87) described as being appropriate for primary school children. These are:

- Information-seeking investigations, such as what happens when eggs hatch?
- Comparing or fair testing, such as which is the better fertiliser for plants?
- Pattern finding, such as do taller trees have more tree rings?
- Hypothesis generating, such as why do echoes appear in some places?
- How-to-do-it investigations, such as how do you build a strong bridge model?

The first four types are exemplified below, with reference to the study of living animals.

## Information seeking

Information seeking might easily be carried out with living animals, as long as the children are made aware of the need to care for the animal in the right ways. One of the misconceptions that children have is that animals need lots of air, so they put them in jars with holes in the lids. Of course, they do need air, but one thing that many small creatures need more is a damp atmosphere, so they may easily dry up if there are too many holes. Looking at minibeasts under a microscope or a strong light also causes them to dry out, so you may need to limit the time they are exposed to heat and light, as well as spraying them with a mist of water from time to time.

## Comparing – ethics and investigation

If children are to investigate and compare living things, then ethics should be one issue to discuss. Children should be encouraged to explore the concept of '**alive**' (see Chapter 8) by comparing themselves and their own feelings to those of other animals. If we are investigating with living animals, what else should children be asked to consider? Some children may have heard of or read about secondary school experiments with worms, such as the experiment to see if worms will grow again if you cut them in half. A better question to ask in the primary school would be, 'How do you think worms would feel if they were cut in half?' A good maxim for guiding experiments and investigations with living animals is that all animals should be returned to their natural environment unharmed after the investigation.

## Pattern finding

Investigations in primary schools that try to find patterns in nature often require planning a fair test, using the word 'fair' in both scientific and human senses. For example, children may think a test is fair when everyone gets a go at doing it. If all the class plants one seed in a pot each, then that would be seen as fair to some children. However, in the scientific sense of the word, the test is fair if all the experimental conditions have been considered and only one variable is allowed to change. This can be very difficult to achieve with living things, since natural conditions are rarely possible to regulate. One way to help children devise ethical investigations is to suggest, 'Ask your animal a question.' Although animals cannot speak their replies to the question, children would be trying to find ways in which the animal could respond with an answer. If, for example, you asked an earthworm, 'Can you hear sounds?' what sort of response could the worm make that would show you that it could hear a sound? Perhaps it would wriggle its body if a loud sound was made nearby? This sort of ethical thinking can help the children to empathise with others (one of the sustainability skills, as well as a value).

This technique could be made fairer by asking more than one earthworm, so a collection of earthworms might be exposed to a sound to see if some of them reacted, or all of them reacted in the same ways. Another way of improving the fairness and finding the pattern in the results would be for children to explore a range of sound-makers to see how they could ensure that the pitch and volume of the sounds was the same for all the tests. They could use a digital sound meter to measure the loudness.

### Hypothesis generating

Minibeasts like woodlice tend to be found in dark, damp places, like underneath rotting logs or in plant debris in the soil. Children should be encouraged to generate hypotheses about why this happens by collecting woodlice and then investigating a number of different environmental conditions. Suggest that the children ask them questions like 'Do you prefer warm, light and dry places or damp, dark and cold places?'

## ICT and minibeasts

Background information on minibeasts can be found in a variety of books (Sherrington 1998, Wenham 1995) or in educational software. Crick software produces CD-ROMs that cover some science for early readers and link the science to the use of Clicker grids. Part of a TEEM (Teachers Evaluating Educational Materials) evaluation of one of these software titles says

> After reading about a minibeast, the user is then given the opportunity to write about the insect. The software offers two differentiated Clicker grids for composing the writing. The pupils' work can be spoken back to them, and printed out and saved in the same manner as when using Clicker independently. As there are two grids available for each insect book, the work can be differentiated for the individual.
>
> (http://www.teem.org.uk/findcdorweb/element/content?element_id=756&content_id=109)

## Simulations and movies

Another useful CD-ROM on insects, *Little Creatures in a Big World*, is from Ransom Publishing. This CD contains some quick time movies showing how important small creatures are in the environmental habitats. I particularly liked the explanation of why dung beetles are so necessary. Try the Ransom website for further information on more recent titles (http://www.ransom.co.uk/). But you also need to use CD-ROMs selectively, if you want to make the most of the learning opportunities in them. Dorling Kindersley produces a CD-ROM about dinosaurs, which features a virtual reality museum and a search for dinosaur bones to bring dinosaurs back to life. As long as children realise that this is a simulation, they will avoid some of the misconceptions that arise from films that show people and dinosaurs living at the same period in history.

## Digital microscopes and minibeasts

Now that digital microscopes are relatively cheap and easy to use, you could examine living minibeasts with one, without doing any damage to the creature. Parts of plants can also be looked at easily. But you should set the investigation into a context of raising questions with the children, so that they focus their observations on finding the answers to these questions. A possible context for using a digital microscope is the question, 'How does a worm manage to move through the soil without any legs or arms?'

One part of the answer is that earthworms have tiny bristles sticking out from their bodies that catch the soil and give them a grip. You can feel these bristles when you hold a worm and the digital microscope enables children to see these fairly easily.

## 5.3 Environments and habitats

### What is a habitat or an environment?

A habitat is a place where living things can live; it provides shelter, food, drink, warmth (or cool in some places), oxygen or other gases needed for life. Most habitats change depending on day and night, seasons or other natural events. Living things respond to changes in their habitats. The environment can be defined in a number of ways – it is sometimes seen as a collection of habitats; it usually includes not only the living things, but also the physical conditions such as light, water and food. According to Anderson (2002: 36) an environment can be:

- a source of energy
- a source of raw materials
- a place to live and shelter
- somewhere to deposit waste

Living things must be adapted to the conditions they live in, but must also be able to cope with changes in these conditions. You can find background science and ideas for environmental science activities in other books, such as Littledyke *et al.* (2000).

### Children's ideas about habitats

A child-friendly way to approach thinking about environments and the concept of a habitat is to start with the child's own environment. Ask questions about where children live, where they feel comfortable, what they need to enjoy their lives, what aspects of the places and people around them they like. Then ask them to think about animals they know about. Animals as pets might be an appropriate starter for some children, while animals in zoos might be more familiar to others. Animals seen on TV or film are another likely source of children's knowledge and attitudes to living things. The SPACE series of books for younger children suggests following up children's ideas by exploring their ideas through topics like shopping (Nuffield Primary Science 1995). For further ideas about using local environments, see Chapter 11: Learning out of school.

### Shopping around for a human habitat

Since one of the life processes is nutrition (or feeding), then shopping can lead children towards an understanding of what they need to stay alive and the ways animals need their environment to stay alive. It can also help children to explore a familiar part of their own environment and the effects human beings have on where they live. A class discussion about local shops, followed by a trip to the shopping area, is a good way to focus children's ideas. A series of sequenced drawings of a trip to the shops (markets, local shops, supermarkets etc.) can help children to compare their ideas to what they really saw and then to consider things like the neighbourhood, streets, pavements, roads, traffic lights, bus stops, waste materials and collection points, types of fresh foods available. Another of the life processes, excretion, can lead us to link the environment with ways in which waste products are treated. Although many local 'recycling' schemes are found in countries across the world, more environmentally friendly 'reuse' schemes are harder to find.

## Designing habitat boxes

Moving on from ourselves to thinking about other animals should involve children in exploring local and more distant places. A more active approach to this is to ask children to design habitat boxes that would be suitable for animals they are investigating. This can be a highly motivated approach, with an open-ended and creative aspect to it. Designs can be made with physical materials, starting with a shoe box, or with virtual materials through drawing programs and clip art. A program that supports this kind of activity is Kid Pix, which allows children to create still or moving pictures from a series of clip art and drawing tools, as well as importing video and still images of their own.

## Circle time

The habitat box activity I saw in a school, with Year 4 children, also involved discussions in circle time about animals and their rights. One question that produced a lot of interesting discussion and argument among the children was, 'Should animals be kept in zoos?' The idea of circle time is that all children have a turn at saying something and their views are all equally important. However, the activity should be a small part of a science lesson, so that there is plenty of time for practical investigations as well as talk. Another way in which ICT can be linked with learning about habitats is through the use of electronic mail to link schools in different parts of the country or the world, to create a virtual circle time activity.

## Young children's ideas about controversial issues

A project that involved student teachers in the USA linking with others in London asked a number of controversial questions, based on ideas from Plant and Firth (1995), such as:

'Is all life sacred (including wasps and bacteria that cause diseases in humans)?'

'Should people be in control of Nature?'

Student teachers then attempted to adapt some of these difficult questions to use with young children between five and six years old. They managed to elicit some interesting ideas from these children. Most of the youngest children related the question, 'Should people be in charge of Nature?' to their own domestic or school surroundings and responded about pets, for example:

*Child C. (age 5)* 'Yes we should. My pet worm likes eating grass but I would like him to eat a chicken sandwich so he would be more like me.'

*Child H. (age 5)* 'Yes. All animals and birds should live in the country.'

*Child Je. (age 6)* 'Half and half really. My cat likes Wiskas but we have to buy her cheaper food.'

But some young children have more sophisticated views and ideas:

*Child Je. (age 6)* 'If it is up to us we might get it all wrong and the animal would be unhappy. They can't speak and tell us what they want so it's difficult to get it right.'

## More complex ideas from young children

In reviewing the original statement, 'Preserving species is not important, since scientists can make new genes', one student changed this to, 'Animals dying out forever, like the dinosaurs, is not important because scientists can make new life in their laboratories. What do you think about this?'

*Child G. (age 5)* There's not many elephants left, you know. Surely scientists couldn't make an elephant in a little laboratory! It is very important to stop animals dying out forever, although some people don't even care about their pets.

*Child C. (age 5)* I don't believe scientists can make a potion strong enough to make a life, so of course it's important to save everything we can.

*Child H. (age 5)* Even if scientists could do this, it still matters.

*Child Jy. (age 5)* Extinction you mean! Yes, it is important to save all animals. It would be good if the scientists could make one but there needs to be one left to show the animal what to do, how to get food and all that.

*Child Ja. (age 6)* Yes, we must keep all animals alive in case the scientist potion goes all wrong and makes a monster instead.

So quite young children can express complex ideas about the relationships between ourselves as humans and the rest of the animal world. What are the implications for teaching? Harlen (2000) is the most useful source of ideas about ways to develop children's ideas through practical work, a focus on words and their meanings, asking questions, encouraging children to ask questions and to investigate answers to their questions, creating links between common events.

## Simple or complex ideas?

In view of the complexity of the ideas of the young children quoted above, some suggested activities about science, environment and the use of ICT might seem rather simplistic. One common computerised scenario for studying habitats is that of a food pyramid, such as the link between grass, rabbits and foxes in a simplified ecosystem. Some of these games can be fun, but they can also prevent children from thinking for themselves and may give too simplistic an idea of how complex natural cycles really are. It can be more educational to get children to act out some of these scenarios, putting themselves into the situation rather than just being the passive recipients of computer software. Social constructivism theory requires children to co-operate with each other, rather than interact with a machine, although smart technologies do seem to simulate the interactions that can help children to learn. TEEM evaluations (http://www.teem.org.uk/subject_profiles/primary_science) from class teachers mention the advantage of children being able to complete activities on their own at the computer – but this is not the only way of using ICT in the classroom or in the computer suite. An important way to help children learn is to take their complex ideas seriously as a starting point for creative solutions to curriculum planning – not just taking ready-made solutions from ICT sources, but using these sources as tools in our own plans for the children in our own classes.

## Summary

In this chapter, you have been introduced to the big idea of education for sustainability, seen how the study of 'ourselves as humans' can be carried out with children, with support from interactive whiteboards for studying nutrition. You have read about ways of studying animals, raising controversial questions and planning ethical investigations, and realised that the complexity of children's ideas can make us question the suitability of using 'ready-made' lesson plans and schemes.

You should now be able to:

- Recognise the knowledge and understanding, skills, values and dispositions of education for sustainability.
- Use digital cameras, microscopes and CD-ROMs to support teaching and learning about ourselves and other animals.
- Draw on children's own experiences and ideas to help you plan lessons to study environments and human effects on them.

## Web links

Local Agenda 21 is the term given to a global action plan for the twenty-first century aimed at delivering sustainable development. This action plan was adopted by nearly 180 of the world's governments at the 1992 Earth Summit in Rio. The agreement is aimed at reversing the negative impact of human behaviour on the environment, and promoting sustainable development in all countries. See for example, this website:

http://www.cornwall.gov.uk/Council-Services/ab-de03/agenda21/agenda21.htm

http://www.teem.org.uk/subject_profiles/primary_science
TEEM stands for Teachers Evaluating Educational Materials. The website is a useful resource to help find suitable software that has been evaluated by teachers, with useful case studies and ideas for working with groups or whole classes in schools. Some evaluations are just of the content of the software; others include classroom context evaluations too.

http://besd.becta.org.uk
This is good for evaluations of software and CD-ROMs.

http://edcompass.smarttech.com/en/learning/activities/notebook.aspx
There are lesson plans available from this website in a format that fits interactive whiteboards. Some are suitable for the UK market while others fit better with the USA and Canada.

www.sciencenetlinks.com
More science websites from the USA.

http://exhibits.pacsci.org/nutrition/sleuth/sleuth.html.
USA-based website on nutrition.

http://www.scienceweb.org.uk/flashindex.html
This website has some free simulations to help deal with aspects of primary science teaching. Some of it is rather simple, but there are some interactive graphics linked to downloadable text-based instructions and worksheets.

http://www.ransom.co.uk/
This commercial company produces CD-ROMs, including *Insects* and *Whale of a Tale*.

http://www.schoolzone.co.uk/evaluations/findeval.htm
Evaluations of software for schools, often written by teachers.

http://www.itsyourgoal.com/
This website offers previews of a piece of software that helps children to explore health and exercise, with a fantasy football focus to it. It aims at science, ICT, PSHE and citizenship at Key Stages 2 and 3.

# 6

# Let there be light

## Introduction

This chapter is about the big ideas of light, colour and vision. It explores how students can plan and teach lessons dealing with complex and abstract concepts concerning light, colour and vision and how to integrate ICT tools within these lessons. Digital cameras, the Internet and interactive whiteboards with projectors are a major focus in one of the lessons described, while paint programs and data logging of light intensity comes into others. Light and shadows are explored in section 6.3, which links to an earlier case study from Chapter 3. Finally, there are some thoughts and ideas about seeing, light and vision.

## Learning objectives

By the end of the chapter, you should be able to help children to:

- Identify sources of light – using the Internet, interactive whiteboard, word banks and data logging tools.
- Explore light and colour – using paint programs, Word, clip art and light meters.
- Understand light and shadows – using digital camera and interactive whiteboard.
- Recognise the importance of light in vision – using digital microscope, interactive whiteboard and the Internet.

**TABLE 6.1  ICT National Curriculum links**

|  | Key Stage 1 (ages 5–7) | Key Stage 2 (ages 8–11) |
|---|---|---|
| Sources of light | 1a, 1b, 2a, 2b | 1a, 1b, 1c, 2a, 3b, 5b |
| Colour and light | 1a, 1b, 2a, 3a | 1b, 2a, 2b, 5b |
| Light and shadows | 1a, 2a, 3a | 2b, 3a |
| Light and vision | 1a, 5b | 1a, 5a |

**TABLE 6.2  QCA scheme links**

|  | Science | ICT |
|---|---|---|
| Sources of light | 1D, 3F, 5E | 1A, 2B, 2C, 6D |
| Colour and light | 1D, 2B | 1A, 2B |
| Light and shadows | 3F, 5E | 3A |
| Light and vision | 2B, 6F | 2E, 6D |

## Light as a big idea in science

Light, or visible light to give it a more accurate name, is a type of '**radiation**' and part of the '**electromagnetic spectrum**' (an even bigger idea), along with things like ultraviolet and infrared radiation, as well as longer and shorter '**wavelengths**' that we call X-rays and radio waves. Another big idea is that we see things when light enters our eyes and the radiation is translated into electrical impulses, which are transmitted to our brains through nerves. What is visible to most humans is not necessarily visible to other animals – that depends on the number and type of light-sensitive cells we have in our eyes. Some of the big ideas about light are presented as simple in some science books, but in modern views of science are much more complex (see misconceptions tables below). For teaching in primary schools, the main ideas that need to be understood are that:

Light exists (but dark does not).

It travels (very fast).

It travels in straight lines (usually).

It can be reflected by some objects (and may then appear to change colour).

It can go through some objects (partially or completely).

It may change direction as it goes through objects (and this can cause magnification).

More background science on light and colour can be found in many of the books in the References and further reading at the end of this book (for example, Johnsey *et al.* 2002, Anderson 2002, Wenham 1995) or, of course, on the Internet.

## 6.1 Sources of light

There are many sources of light in our world as well as light sources in the universe. At the level of the universe, the main sources are the stars, of which our sun is one. One of the common misconceptions here is that although light is emitted from some objects, some children think light comes from others because it is reflected from them. Ask children to draw pictures of things they think produce light, then help them to compare and discuss these, so that they begin to recognise the difference between light emitters and other secondary sources. They could try to organise the sources they identify into categories, such as hot light sources (candles or bonfires), or light they may associate with living things (fireflies or cats' eyes). A mirror or the moon would be considered as secondary sources of light, since they reflect light from original sources. Children could collect pictures of light sources from newspapers and magazines, or the Internet or clip art collections.

### Measuring light

However, a more correct viewpoint would be that the light we see in the sky really originates in many different sources on the earth as well as the sun and the stars. People illuminate the planet with road lights, buildings and so forth while natural light from the earth comes from lightning, volcanoes, the aurora borealis, phosphorescence etc. Children should be challenged to think of where the light in the sky comes from before it gets to the sky. If you can get hold of a light meter (try LogIT Explorer for a fairly simple digital light meter), ask children to explore different parts of the room to see where the brightest parts are – hence where most light is coming from. Ask them what they think the light meter is doing. If you only have light meters without data logging software, try recording some of the data on a spreadsheet.

**TABLE 6.3** Misconceptions about light sources

| |
|---|
| **Common misconception** Light comes from the sky. |
| **Usual age for misconception** 5–8 years. |
| **The scientific explanation** Light does come from a number of different sources, but the simple scientific view is that the sky transmits light originating from the sun or the stars. |
| **Ways to address the misconception** Children should be challenged to think of where the light in the sky comes from before it gets to the sky. They should be encouraged to think of where the light from a mirror comes from before it reaches the mirror or where the moon's light comes from. |

**TABLE 6.4** Misconceptions about light travelling

| |
|---|
| **Common misconception** Light does not move, it just is there or it is not there. |
| **Usual age for misconception** 5–8 years. |
| **The scientific explanation** Light travels (quickly, in fact it is the fastest thing in the universe at 300 million metres per second or 186,000 miles per second), but it goes so quickly that we do not see it moving. |
| **Ways to address the misconception** How far away is the sun? How far the moon? How far away are the nearest stars? These questions might help children to think about light travelling from these objects. Another more practical activity is to ask them to observe a candle burning and draw what happens to the light from the candle. |

## Light travels in straight lines

Well, mostly it does, unless it travels past a very massive object when gravity seems to be able to make it bend. This was predicted by Einstein and was shown to be observable during an eclipse of the sun. Light from distant stars was observed to be bent away from their expected positions as the light passed close to the sun. This was only observable when the moon during a solar eclipse blocked the light from the sun itself.

## 6.2 Colour and light

### Seeing colours

The science of colour is complex. Light itself is a part of the electromagnetic spectrum known as visible light, but even this is problematic, since not all humans can see the same things, so not all the colours in the spectrum are visible to all people. Colour blindness is more common in men than in women, due to differences in the colour receptor cells in the retina of the eye. Some animals can see different parts of the spectrum from human vision (e.g. infrared or **ultraviolet**).

### Primary light and primary colours

We sometimes think of the three primary colours as being red, blue and yellow and while this is true for colours in pigments and paints, it is not true for colours in light. The primary light colours are red, blue and green – when these three lights are added together, white light appears. When the three primary pigments are added together, they should produce black. This is because we see light reflected from pigments. The pigment absorbs light. Look up the kids' Ask Jeeves site for more explanations about primary colours and primary lights (www.ajkids.com).

## Some other ideas for investigating light and colour

Children set up simple investigations to explore vision, such as colour vision, camouflage, tunnel vision, left/right eye dominance, optical illusions and what people can/cannot see. Use paint-type programs to support the set-up.

Investigate the effect of three colour torches to make white light. http://www.continental.clara.net/physics/colMix.htm is a site that provides a fascinating simulation on mixing the three primary light colours.

Show children how to design and make a colour wheel, using primary colours (red, blue and green) or primary pigments (red, blue and yellow) and their own choices.

Let them make two colour wheels and test them in pairs to see which makes the lightest shade, nearest to white.

Help children use light boxes and coloured bricks or other materials to see which shows up best in dim light. This has safety implications for clothing to wear at night. You could make a light box from a cereal packet, by cutting a small hole in it that children could see into and another small hole where the light enters. The second hole can then be covered with different materials to alter the amount or the colour of the light entering the box.

Use a set of colour filters to look at coloured objects in order to see what effects these filters have on the colours. The explanation of the effect is complex but involves the idea of a filter acting like a gate to stop some of the light passing through. So a blue filter stops red and green light from passing through and only allows blue light through.

## 6.3 Light and shadows

### Logging light intensity

'How much light and how much dark?' is a question that can be answered through use of ICT – data-logging kits these days usually come with a light meter. A simple one to use is LogIT Explorer, which can be used as a stand-alone, hand-held device or can be linked to a computer. You can lead in to this through cameras, where the amount of light falling on the lens determines the type of picture. Most modern cameras have a built-in light meter, so that the flash comes on automatically – this is the link to science in everyday life.

### Creative uses of light meters

Feasey and Gallear (2001: 35) suggest using light meters or data-logging tools to measure light reflected from a set of mirrors for Key Stage 2 children, so that they can compare the difference between light reflected from new or scratched mirrors. Although this should work, it would probably be obvious to children that new shiny mirrors would work better than old scratched ones, so the purpose of using ICT here would just be to prove the obvious and to practise using ICT tools. It would be far better to find a

**TABLE 6.5** Misconceptions about shadows

| |
|---|
| **Common misconception** Shadows are the same as reflections. |
| **Usual age for misconception** 5–8 years. |
| **The scientific explanation** A shadow is the absence of light caused by the light being blocked by a solid object. A reflection is the light reflected from an object on a shiny surface and back again from the surface. |
| **Ways to address the misconception** Children should be encouraged to draw their shadows as well as drawing round their shadows then compare what they expected to see (i.e. their drawings) with what they really see. Digital photos of their shadows and themselves can be used to make these comparisons more clear. |

**TABLE 6.6** More misconceptions about shadows

| |
|---|
| **Common misconception** Shadows move in the same direction as the light source. |
| **Usual age for misconception** 5–8 years. |
| **The scientific explanation** The shadow moves in the opposite direction to the movement of the source of light, because light travels in straight lines. |
| **Ways to address the misconception** Close observation of the position of the sun and the change in the shadow's position would be one way of dealing with this, but since the change is slow, it is not so successful with younger children. Another way would be to use a torch to illuminate an object and move the torch left or right, while looking at the shadow position. |

situation where the answer was unknown, or at least not so obvious, so that children could be more involved in investigation, creativity and real science. Perhaps they could try to find out which clothes would be seen more easily in dark places, so that they would be safer walking home from school on winter evenings? What other creative ideas could you come up with to link light intensity with a purpose? Do plants grow better in high light intensities? Is that too obvious?

I recognised the following misconception when working with a group of seven-year-olds growing beans on a window sill in the classroom. One of them thought that the shadow would move the same way as the sun, not the opposite way.

But as usual with misconceptions, you cannot just teach the right answers – you need to provide a number of experiences and keep returning to them through discussions until the child is ready to make the intellectual leap, while keeping good records of the progress they are making.

Ask children, 'Draw yourself and the sun and show where your shadow would be and what it would look like.' Then let them go outside on a sunny day with a partner and have their friend draw round their shadow – then let one of them lie on the ground and have their partner draw around them. Compare the differences now.

## 6.4  How do we see?

### Models of vision

From the research evidence (Osborne *et al.* 1993), it seems that there are three common models that children have to explain vision and light. One is the sea of light model – that there needs to be light in the room or the environment and then we just see by looking at something. A second common model is that we see just by looking and that our eyes send out something, which hits the object, and then we see it – rather like the idea of Superman and his X-ray eyes from science fiction comics and films. The third is a mixture of active and passive eye. Light comes into our eyes but we also have to be looking at the object – which is very close to the scientific explanation, that says we just need light to enter our eyes. But then, of course, what we see is not the same as what we think we see, as training is needed in order to translate the image into a recognisable and meaningful item. So a scientist looking at a photograph from an electron microscope will see the same image as a layperson, but will recognise many different things in it.

### Digital microscopes

The Intel QX3 computer microscope is intended for use by parents and children from the age of six years. Although the set-up can be a problem (the version I used needed Windows 98 and refused to work with Windows NT), it does give good pictures of items like salt and sugar crystals, with magnifications of 10×, 60× and 200×. The interesting aspect of the microscope from the vision angle is that it provides either top or bottom lighting. This emphasises the concept that the light has to strike an opaque object and then reflect off it into the microscope tube in order for the microscope to 'see' and then put the image onto the computer screen. However, with an object viewed with light from beneath, the light comes up below the object and then you really see the shadow of the object on the computer screen.

### Looking at things

How does light help the people to see the objects? Research from the SPACE project (Osborne *et al.* 1993) suggested that if a light source is clearly identifiable in the situation, children are likely to identify light as being necessary to see. However, in situations where the light source is not so obvious, for example, when someone is sitting in a room and looking at a book with just the natural light from the windows, then they are more likely to just say 'we see with our eyes' and ignore the need for light.

### Comparing eyes

It is useful to ask children to compare their own eyes with those of someone else in the class. In this activity the idea of similarities and differences in observations is important. But if you might want to stress that the things that make us all human should be much more important than the things that make us all different, and refer to PSHE, citizenship, anti-racism and ethos here. The QCA ICT scheme Unit 2E suggests some activities about comparing human characteristics and entering the data in a database – this is suggested for children in Year 2 (i.e. aged about seven years):

> Prepare data for a database on eye colour, amongst other aspects of ourselves – this criterion is a fixed one, while others are changeable, e.g. height or length of hair.

## Animal eyes

Try starting from questions like these:

Where are your eyes?

Do animals see in the same way?

Where are rabbits' eyes?

Why do most living things have two eyes, not just one or four or many?

Are insect eyes the same as ours?

Use a Big Book to help children observe the eyes of different animals and engage in discussion and comparison. Alternatively, use a CD-ROM of animals or the Internet for clips of animals and perhaps videos too. Our eyes are at the front of our heads, while many animals have eyes at the sides of their heads – ask children to think about hunters as opposed to hunted animals. Think about nature programmes you have seen on TV – deer versus cheetah, bison versus wolves. What about crocodiles with eyes on the tops of their heads?

## Summary

In this chapter, you have seen how children can identify and explore light sources; how colour can be explored through activities with torches and through simulations found on the Internet. You looked at some common misconceptions about light and shadows and about how we see and how spreadsheets can help children handle data and make scientific predictions.

You should now be able to:

- Plan lessons about sources and effects of light, such as shadows and reflections.
- Support children's learning through the use of open-ended questions and resources.
- Recognise some of the background science about light, vision and colour, and be able to find more sources of science knowledge in this area.

## Web links

www.ajkids.com
Search engine for children.

http://www.technologystudent.com/designpro/pricol1.htm
Information about colour and light.

http://www.continental.clara.net/physics/colMix.htm
A fascinating simulation of primary colours.

CHAPTER

# Science and technology in everyday life

## Introduction

This chapter is about ways in which we can teach science and ICT in school and use everyday life for contexts and good examples for children to learn from. There are cross-curriculum links, especially with design/technology and history. Four areas of everyday life are selected and the chapter shows how to plan activities to deal with them. Through the home context, there are links to the QTT standard about parents and carers. Creative aspects include making traffic light models through the context of electricity; using drama and role play to teach electricity concepts; and making direct contact with scientists through email.

## Learning objectives

By the end of the chapter you will be able to plan and teach aspects of the following areas of science, using the ICT tools described:

- Kitchen chemistry – using PowerPoint and Word.
- Electricity – using Clicker software, an interactive whiteboard and other tools.
- The supermarket – using data-logging hardware and software, the Internet etc.
- Real scientists – using Internet searches and email.

TABLE 7.1    ICT National Curriculum links

|  | Key Stage 1 (ages 5–7) | Key Stage 2 (ages 8–11) |
|---|---|---|
| Kitchen chemistry | 1a, 2c, 2d, 3b, 5b | 1a, 1b, 5a |
| Electricity | 1b, 2a, 3a | 1b, 2a, 2b |
| Supermarket science | 1a, 3a | 1c, 2a, 4a |
| Real scientists | 1a, 3a | 1b, 2c, 3a, 5a, 5b |

**TABLE 7.2   QCA scheme links**

|  | Science | ICT |
|---|---|---|
| Kitchen chemistry | 1C, 2D, 3C, 4D, 5D, 6C | 1B, 4A |
| Electricity | 2F, 4F, 6G | 1B, 5E |
| The supermarket | 1B, 2E, 3A, 3B, 5A, 6B | 5D, 5F, 6D |
| Real scientists | 2A, 3E, 5A | 2C, 3E, 4A, 6D |

## Why is learning in everyday life a big idea?

In May 2003, the UK Government produced a document called the *Primary National Strategy* (http://www.standards.dfes.gov.uk/primary/) in which six core principles for teaching and learning were introduced – one of these was:

> Develop learning skills and personal qualities across the curriculum, inside and outside the classroom.
>
> (http://www.standards.dfes.gov.uk/seu/coreprinciples2/)

## Science and everyday life

Science teaching is supposed to use everyday contexts so that children can see the connections between science at school and their own lives:

> Science stimulates and excites pupils' curiosity about phenomena and events in the world around them ... Through science, pupils understand how major scientific ideas contribute to technological change – impacting on industry, business and medicine and improving quality of life.
>
> (DfEE 1999: 76)

One way in which everyday contexts can help children to learn is by providing them with reasons for learning. Motivation is an important part of teaching in school and an even more important part of why we learn things out of school. In science lessons, we should try to interest and motivate the children by providing them with cross-curricular contexts in which they can use their own prior knowledge and experience and then extend these experiences.

But there can be problems since a lot of the science and technology we use in everyday lives is so complex or so hidden that it is not easy to link it with school science. One of the aims of this chapter is to make the connections between science and technology in school and some aspects of everyday life that children themselves do experience, rather than the experiences which adults think that children have.

## ICT and everyday life

Many adults use ICT tools as part of their everyday lives. Some children use ICT as part of their leisure activities. ICT in the school should provide experiences that fulfil both of these roles – it should be fun, if possible, and it should provide tools similar to those that adults use to help them carry out their tasks more effectively and efficiently.

## 7.1 Kitchen chemistry

In our homes, we use many chemicals without thinking much about them, unless we are dieting or trying to avoid additives. Children too will usually have had experience of some of the common chemicals, such as salt and sugar. There are many opportunities to link the everyday chemicals in kitchens with the science that children can study practically in school. The suggestions in this section are linked to ideas in Chapter 9 about materials and particles via the question, 'What if the chair was made from chocolate?' Ideas about change in state, such as chocolate melting if you actually made it into a chair and sat on it, link with the activity of heating and burning sugar, so chemistry and physics are combined in the first activity.

### Safety first

Most chemicals can be dangerous if swallowed; even common salt can make you sick – avoid all tasting in these investigations, unless you are sure it is safe.

Some chemicals are fire hazards (e.g. white or methylated spirit and potassium permanganate). Some give off dangerous vapours. Others can have long-term harmful effects, like lead, asbestos and mercury.

Check with local authority or school guidelines if you are unsure of policy about using chemicals.

### Burning tests

Ensure that children have no loose ends, such as hair, scarves, ties, if they are dealing with fire. Use a burning tray, a metal oven dish with sand in it, a small piece of candle in a plasticene holder and a wooden peg-type holder. Avoid electric hotplates or spirit burners. Avoid areas where children move around a lot. Avoid the use of paper near the burning tray. Always have an adult in attendance when burning takes place. Try to find alternatives to glass wherever possible, for example, using cooking foil containers for hot experiments or plastic containers for cool experiments. Granulated sugar can be heated fairly safely in small foil containers over a candle flame. Children should be encouraged to use the senses of smell and hearing, as well as vision, to observe the events that take place as the material changes. Other types of sugar could be compared, before they use sugars and other chemicals in cooking investigations. Although children are sometimes helped to make cakes, they do not often use these situations as science investigations. A creative teacher could manage to include science as well as design/technology in a cake-making session, where different amounts of ingredients are used and the final products sampled for taste preferences.

Another relatively simple test within kitchen chemistry is for acidity or pH. You can use litmus paper for acid or alkali testing, but universal indicator paper gives much more accurate results. A more interesting colour indicator can be made by boiling some red cabbage and using the blue liquid that results from this. This liquid turns pink in acid but also gives some interesting green colours when exposed to alkaline chemicals.

The kinds of chemical found in the kitchen that are relatively safe to test include sugars, salt, raising agents like cream of tartar and bicarbonate of soda, weak acids such as lemon juice, vinegar and citric acid, and some types of soap and detergent. But some children may be allergic to detergents, so take care and if in doubt use disposable plastic gloves.

## 7.2 Electricity

The topic of electricity can be dealt with by children of any age in the primary school or even within the nursery if it is kept at the right level of concrete activities versus abstract concepts. To study electricity as a whole-class activity requires a lot of resources, so it may be easier to try it out with a small group. A good starting point is to examine battery-operated devices, such as torches or toys, and then take them apart to see where the batteries are and how they seem to be connected to the working parts of the device, like the bulb in a torch or the motor in a toy car.

### Lighting up a bulb

Ask the children to be creative and suggest different ways to make a bulb light up, using the absolute minimum of equipment. The answer is that you need one wire, one bulb and one battery, plus some ingenuity. There are four different configurations that will result in the bulb lighting up. The main learning objective in children building circuits is that they recognise the need for two connections to the battery and two to the bulb. So in the above problem, one part of the bulb needs to touch one part of the battery, while the wire is used to connect the other part of the bulb to the other part of the battery. But which parts are the crucial connectors?

### Adapting to everyday life contexts

How would you adapt the lesson for children aged around 11 years to help them explore traffic lights? It is possible to make simple switches with just a couple of paper fasteners in a piece of card and a paper clip to join them up. Three of these home-made switches would be enough to link up with three bulbs (covered by red, amber and yellow coloured filters) and then a battery to simulate the traffic light system. Try to fit it into a scheme of work for making and testing traffic lights, so linking science with design/technology. What would children need to be able to do, in order to make and test the traffic light circuits and then link the circuit to a control and timing system, using ICT control Lego or a similar technical kit?

## Batteries and cells

You should be aware that the 1.5 volt batteries are technically known as '**cells**' – a single cell gives 1.5 volts while collections of cells should be called 'batteries' and give voltages of 3, 4.5 or 6 volts etc. This arises from the technical word for a collection of guns, called a 'battery'. However, for the younger children, the common term 'battery' is more appropriate.

ICT applications that might be used in electricity include:

- Using a word bank to help children record their ideas and learn how to write and spell the specialist words they will have learnt to say and hear.

- A digital camera would also be useful to support children's ideas, as they could take photos of circuits they have made and demonstrate the ways in which they put together the components to make lights work.

- Paint-type programs to help them draw the components and diagrams of what they did and how they linked things together.

- Writing frames prepared by the teacher to support them in describing their actions and what they found out.

- Writing and drawing frames to support their homework assignments.

- *Clicker 4* is a software program originally designed for use in special education which can be adapted easily to support children's writing in the activity about electricity.

## Analogies and electricity

Analogies about electricity can be useful, but they can also lead to misconceptions, for example, 'Electricity is like water flowing in the pipes around your house.' It is not really like that at all, but the analogy is commonly used and can lead to further misconceptions. A more useful analogy for electricity making a motor work is that of a bicycle. The cyclist represents the source of energy – the battery – as the energy she uses is stored in her muscles and originates from the chemicals in food. When she cycles, she transfers her energy to the chain, which represents the wires in the circuit. The movement of the chain represents the electricity. The wheel that turns and pushes the bike along the path represents the motor in an electrical circuit that uses electrical energy and turns it into movement.

**TABLE 7.3** Misconceptions about electricity

| |
|---|
| **Common misconception 1** You only need one connection between the battery and the device to make it work. |
| **Usual age for misconception** 5–9 years. |
| **The scientific explanation** You need two, but sometimes it is not obvious since the two wires may be linked together in one piece of flex. One contact is with the positive, the other with the negative terminal of the battery. |
| **Ways to address the misconception** Children need to experience making connections with very simple equipment, not just with kits that hide the actual connections. Battery and bulb holders make it easy to construct models, but often hide the ways in which the connections are really being made. |
| **Common misconception 2** A battery stores electricity. |
| **Usual age for misconception** 7–11 years. |
| **The scientific explanation** It does not – but it does store energy, in the form of chemical bonds. The chemicals inside a battery react with each other when the battery is connected up in a circuit. Electricity is the form of energy that is produced from this reaction, as well as energy in the form of heat. |
| **Ways to address the misconception** Examine the different types of battery that are available, not by cutting them up, but by looking at the lists of chemicals inside them. Lithium batteries are now common for use in digital cameras and other devices. |

## 7.3 Science in the supermarket

A visit to the supermarket must be one of the most common adult experiences and one that is familiar to children from an early age. This section explores some of the science and technology used in supermarkets and demonstrates how activities in schools can be linked to them. The focus is on food and associated technology although there is a brainstorm included to help you introduce ideas about the use of a supermarket context for teaching and learning more generally.

### Supermarkets on the internet

A trip to the supermarket with a group or whole class can usually be arranged easily – many supermarket managers are keen to support educational visits and some supermarket chains produce educational materials for schools and teachers. Try visiting Sainsbury's website for information about this and then compare it with other supermarket chains (http://www.j-sainsbury.co.uk/csr/community.htm). The virtual museum at Sainsbury's is worth a look as it links history with science, ICT and technology and may be useful for teaching in Key Stage 2.

Try the Tesco site (http://www.tesco.com/corporateinfo/) for information about the Tesco computers for schools initiative as an example of the way in which larger companies translate their policies of Corporate Social Responsibility (CSR) into support for schools. Asda supermarkets' website has a section for education: 'Welcome to the ASDA Big Healthy Body, an exciting new way for children, teachers and parents to learn about healthy living. There are many different areas to explore and enjoy inside the Big Healthy Body' (www.asda.co.uk). Part of this site contains downloadable activities in science for children in primary schools, some of it linked to Science Year 2002.

> As part of the ASDA Big Healthy Body initiative, children are invited to take part in activity learning trails at their local ASDA store or depot. Teachers accompany the children on the visit, where they are met by an ASDA Colleague and escorted around the store or depot on a specially constructed route. Children fill in trail activity worksheets and take part in fun demonstrations, helping them to place being healthy in a practical context.

Safeway supermarkets also have a website where they provide information about their CSR, showing their involvement with local communities (http://www.safeway.co.uk).

## Visit a farm

One of the interesting educational links is a farm visit scheme, through the LEAF (Linking Environment and Farming) organisation. Several supermarkets work with LEAF (www.leafuk.org) who organise such visits.

## Spreadsheets and supermarkets

The QCA scheme Unit 5D integrated task for ICT suggests an activity about using spreadsheets for calculating the quantities of materials needed to make different numbers of biscuits (QCA 2003: 60–61). A supermarket visit could provide the opportunity to collect information about the costs of different biscuit packets and lead in to this QCA activity in an everyday context. A science lesson could then be the context for testing the cooking of different ingredients that make biscuits.

## Brainstorming more ideas for ICT and science activities arising from a supermarket visit

■ Explore the ways the supermarket uses ICT in food management, customer services, finance and ordering stock, weighing and bar code readers.

■ Use data-logging hardware to take measurements of the temperatures in different parts of the store. Supermarkets need to check the temperatures in their cool shelves and freezers to ensure that food is kept fresh. Children can check these temperatures with simple equipment like LogIT explorer.

■ How do the doors work? Can you make similar systems using equipment in the school, such as sensors and electrical devices?

- Are there lifts with electronic eyes? Can the children make use of the Roamers in the school, which are supplied in some cases with sensors so that they respond to sounds or to touch? If such Roamers are not available in the school, could teachers borrow them from teacher training institutions?

- There are examples of posters and print everywhere in supermarkets, not just for advertising but also on packaging. Children can use these as starting points for their own designs advertising food and other products and using the ICT resources in school to make similar eye-catching posters. There is an obvious link here with parts of the National Literacy Strategy.

- Is the supermarket an example of sustainable development or does it provide too much packaging? Most supermarket Corporate Social Responsibility web pages will provide evidence of this part of their activities.

- Are the butcher and fishmonger counters better than the pre-packed shelves or just the same? How much variety is there in the fresh counters as compared with the pre-packaged shelves?

- How can you be sure that the food is fresh? Why is the sell-by date different from the use-by date?

- How far does the food come from?

- Is there a seasonal difference between the foods available?

- Can you buy Brussels sprouts in May?

- Can you buy strawberries in January?

- Can you grow some of these food plants in the classroom?

## 7.4  Real scientists

One part of this section is about children actually contacting scientists; the other is about using the Internet in a computer suite to find information about scientists.

### Contacting women scientists

There are a number of ways in which you could go about this – one is to go to the 'Ask an expert' section of a website and post in your question, which will eventually get an answer from a scientist. This may take quite some time, though, and will not usually result in much real contact with the scientist. Another way is to use your ingenuity and personal contacts like Anne Hafford did in the project she set up for her class in a Tower Hamlets, London, primary school (Hafford and Meadows 1999). Anne was teaching groups of five- to seven-year-olds and wanted to use the newly set up Internet connection in her school to support International Women's Day celebrations. So she made contact with a scientist friend who was able to use his contacts in the science community through email. Anne then used email herself to ask these women scientists to field questions from her class. The questions and answers came through the email connection that only worked in the head teacher's office, so small groups of children, under the supervision of another class teacher, came and went into the room to carry out the project. Although the children themselves set the questions, a teacher carried out the actual typing, as at that time they were unable to prepare messages off line and then send them as attachments. The messages received from the scientists were discussed in whole-class sessions and further questions then prepared and sent off. As these were personal contacts, replies were received within a day or two, so children 'responded with enthusiasm and excitement as each new message arrived' (Hafford and Meadows 1999: 21).

## Cross-curriculum approaches to email

The project objectives concerned science and English National Curriculum targets, as well as personal and social education – aiming to encourage children to recognise and celebrate women's achievements and contribution to science. If the project were to run again today, the children would also be carrying out some ICT activities themselves and so there would be ICT objectives to add to the list. One of the difficulties about email projects is the uncertainty of receiving replies regularly. This is not easy to achieve unless you can make personal contacts with the organiser of the email project you are engaged with. There is help available through the British Council for teachers who wish to make contacts using email and set up projects like the one briefly described above – this website is Windows on the World:

> Windows on the World is a free, easy-to-use resource for schools and colleges seeking international links. Teachers can search the database for details of thousands of schools worldwide and may register their own school details for others to view.

> (http://www.wotw.org.uk/)

## Using computer suites

There are special considerations needed when you teach in a computer suite (see Chapter 3 for a case study of a student teacher using a computer suite). As many primary schools now use computer suites, there is a need for teachers to be able to operate in such environments. However, there seems to be no specific standard computer suite – some are adapted from spare rooms or old music rooms, while others may have been purpose built. One of the best comments I heard about computer suites came from a school inspector who suggested that computer suites should be designed with the children in mind, not the needs of the computer manufacturer or even the teacher. He preferred computer suites to look imaginative, perhaps a bit like the science fiction films that children might be familiar with. Not many schools are yet as creative in the displays they put into these rooms as they are with older-style classrooms. One way to use a computer suite would be to support children in looking up information about real scientists and helping them to learn more about what scientists do.

A computer suite would ideally contain:

- Networked computers – high specification and fast machines, with access to
- Networked printers (in colour) and fast access to the
- Internet (Broadband but with a firewall system so that unsuitable materials are blocked), as well as
- Table-top space, so that children can use pencil and paper alongside the screens, and
- Interactive whiteboard, so that the teacher can provide central input into the lesson, while the
- Projector is situated above the children's head, hanging from the ceiling and out of the way of accidents.
- Sound and video links should also be available, both for the whole class and for individuals, through
- Headphones, so that children can access individualised learning packages without disturbing others.

## Summary

In this chapter, you have looked at everyday contexts that can support children's learning about both science and ICT. You saw how a kitchen could be used as a starting point for science investigations; how learning about electricity and control technology could be set in the context of traffic lights; how supermarkets could provide opportunities for learning about food; and how to use the Internet to study the lives of real scientists.

You should now be able to:

- Plan and teach aspects of kitchen chemistry, taking safety into consideration when carrying out more dangerous activities involving heat.
- Understand how to plan lessons in which children learn about electricity in everyday contexts, recognising some of their common misconceptions.
- Recognise the opportunities provided by supermarkets as good environments for investigating the uses of science and technology.
- Use ICT tools to help children make contacts with real scientists and learn about their lives.

## Web links

http://www.standards.dfes.gov.uk/primary/
May 2003 The Primary Strategy.

http://www.curriculumonline.gov.uk/
Curriculum online – a Government site providing teachers with access to a range of resources to support teaching.

http://www.standards.dfes.gov.uk/seu/coreprinciples2/
May 2003 The Core Principles of teaching and learning.

http://www.ictadvice.org.uk/
BECTa advice on ICT including 'Ask an expert'.

http://www.wotw.org.uk/
Window on the world – a British Council site for international links between schools and colleges.

http://www.cricksoft.com/uk/about_us/index.htm?href=/uk/about_us/press/reviews/clicker.htm
Clicker software.

www.leafuk.org
Linking environment and farming.

http://www.jennermuseum.com/overview/index.shtml
A great resource on Edward Jenner, which even has interactive games for children to play.

www.asda.co.uk
Asda supermarkets website.

http://www.safeway.co.uk
Safeway website.

http://www.j-sainsbury.co.uk/csr/community.htm

http://www.j-sainsbury.co.uk/csr/comm_education.htm
Try Sainsbury's websites for information about their educational services.

http://www.tesco.com/corporateinfo/
Tesco website.

# 8

# Energy

## Introduction

This chapter is about the big idea of energy. It is identified in the Key Stage 3 Science National Curriculum as one of the five main themes. Although it is no longer specifically identified in Key Stages 1 or 2, energy underpins many of the other concepts introduced, such as life processes, electricity and sound. The chapter activities aim to introduce some scientific and ICT activities that lead children towards an understanding of energy, through the themes of forces, movements, living things and food.

## Learning objectives

By the end of this chapter you should be able to teach aspects of:

- Forms and transformations of energy – using digital temperature and light sensors, word processing, clip art and digital cameras.
- Forces and movement – using a spreadsheet and light gate sensors.
- Food and energy – using the Internet and data logging.
- The concept of being alive – using clip art, CD-ROMs, databases and interactive whiteboards.

**TABLE 8.1  ICT National Curriculum links**

|  | Key Stage 1 (ages 5–7) | Key Stage 2 (ages 8–11) |
|---|---|---|
| Types and transformations | 2a, 3a, 4b | 1a, 1b, 3a, 3b |
| Forces and movement | 1a, 1b | 1b, 2b, 2c |
| Food and energy | 1a, 3a | 1a, 2b, 5a, 5b |
| The concept of 'alive' | 1b, 3b, 5a | 1a, 1b, 2a, 3a |

**TABLE 8.2   QCA scheme links**

|  | Science | ICT |
|---|---|---|
| Types and transformations | 1B, 1D, 2F, 4F | 1B, 2B, 3A |
| Forces and movement | 1E, 2E, 4E | 3C, 5D, 5F |
| Food and energy | 1E, 2E, 4A, 5A | 5B, 5F, 6D |
| The concept of 'alive' | 1A, 2B, 4A, 6A | 1C, 1D, 3B, 5B |

## Why is energy a big idea?

In the Science National Curriculum for primary schools in England and Wales, energy is not mentioned specifically, because it is considered too abstract, although many aspects of it are covered. So children do study forces, electricity, sound and light, which are all part of the concept of energy.

## Energy and work

One big idea is that energy enables you to do work. The concept of work is easily mis-construed, since the scientific meaning of the term is very different from its everyday meanings. In science, work is done when a force moves through a distance and more work, therefore, means more force or more distance. Children may know that their parents/carers and older siblings may 'go out to work' in order to earn money. They may also think that some of their own actions in school constitute 'work' and that the products of their activities are also called work, as in 'Hand in your work at the end of the lesson.'

## Types of energy

Another big idea is that energy can be transformed, or changed from one form into another, but that it cannot be used up. So we can think of energy as being of different types, which can be interchanged. These include heat, light, sound, electricity and maybe fuel and food too, although some purists might argue about the precise mean-ings and definitions. One way of thinking about transformations is to consider how a torch works – what happens when passing electricity through it lights up a bulb? The energy in the chemicals inside the battery ('cell' in purist scientific terms) is trans-formed into electricity, then into heat and light in the bulb. An electric motor is another example used in primary school teaching – the energy from the electricity is changed into movement energy in the motor, along with some sound and heat energy too.

## Energy resources

We often think of ways in which we generate electricity as using energy resources. So these could include fossil fuels, like coal, petrol and gas, so-called non-renewable energy resources, as well as solar, wind and wave, so-called renewable resources. 'Renewable' is a relative term, depending on the timescale in which you think. Eventually, coal and gas reserves will run out, but eventually the sun will also 'run out' in the sense that all the hydrogen in it will have decayed to helium. It just happens on a different timescale.

## Energy and people

Energy is a human idea invented to help us understand the complexity of relationships between things and events in everyday life. But you cannot see energy, you cannot describe it as having a shape or a colour, it is not inside an object. Yet we often talk about having lots of energy, feeling that we lack energy when we are tired or that eating certain foods gives you energy. There is a feeling among some science educators that teachers should know a lot of background science in order to be able to teach primary science well. While this is true up to a point, it is also true that science is an area of study that changes rapidly and concepts of energy (along with those about time and space etc.) do not remain constant. So is it better for teachers to keep an open mind about some of these more controversial concepts in science? We may find that some of the ideas that children have which we call misconceptions now may, in a few years' time, turn out to be correct science after all. We still use Newtonian concepts in teaching many physical science concepts even though these have been superseded by other theories.

## 8.1 Types and transformations of energy

The idea of energy is a complex one and very abstract. However, children can be taught through concrete activities about the many different types of energy they are aware of in their everyday lives, such as sound, light, fuels and electricity. Most children will know the word 'energy' and its everyday meaning and some will already have started to form a concept of energy as an overarching idea associated with sustainable development and conservation. Some aspects of energy transformations can be taught through the use of ICT, especially through a variety of websites (see a search of Ask Jeeves http://www.ask.co.uk), but practical activities in science can also be supported through ICT tools such as digital measuring devices. Since light and heat are forms of energy, it is relatively simple to set up situations where the amounts of light and heat can be measured.

## Role play with electricity

One of the other ways of getting children to think about energy transformations is to engage them in some role play, as I once observed a student teacher doing with a class of six- and seven-year-olds. Try this out with a whole class once the children have had some practical experience of making things work, for example, after letting them make simple circuits with batteries, bulbs, wires, motor buzzers and bells. Prepare some poster resources, with symbols (or pictures of the objects for younger children) for the various components that children have used. Arrange the children in a circle with their feet touching, to simulate a complete circuit. Then discuss with them the idea that they represent the wires in the circuit and that those with the posters represent the components. The concept of electricity flowing round the circuit can be represented by a series of balls that the children pass on, one to the next. These represent the electrons flowing through the wire, although the concept of invisible electrons is probably too difficult to explain in the primary school. The fact that the children's feet are touching is meant to represent the idea that the circuit must be unbroken if the electricity is to flow. When the ball arrives at a component, encourage the children to make the appropriate response, demonstrating the effect of the energy from the electricity being transformed into kinetic energy (movement) in a motor, sound energy in a bell or buzzer, or light (and heat) energy in a bulb. Once they have enjoyed the simulations and role play, you can suggest to smaller groups ways of recording what they did and what it meant, using ICT tools such as word processing and clip art.

### Children recording for an audience

This recording activity should be set in a meaningful context – there should be a purpose to it, such as making a display for other children to see, for parents' evening or for an assembly. One successful way of motivating children to produce good records is to let them show their products to younger children. The idea that they can teach others through their own outcomes makes it more worthwhile than just recording things for the teacher to mark. This idea of an audience for children's writing and drawing is an important one in every area of their activities.

## 8.2 Forces and movement

Forces in the primary school are usually studied through practical activities involving pushes and pulls. Children aged five to seven should be taught 'about the movement of familiar things, that both pushes and pulls are examples of forces and to recognise that when things speed up, slow down or change direction there is a cause' (DfEE 1999: 81).

### The concept of acceleration

There are three effects of forces that need to be understood, all involving changes in movement, not just movement itself. This is one of the major causes of misconceptions in both children and adults. Many people think that for an object to be moving, there must be a force acting on it. It was Aristotle who first explored this idea, and Newton who expressed the notion that forces cause changes in movement, so speeding up, slowing down or changing direction. The problem is that in our everyday lives, unseen forces do slow things down, so movements do not continue forever. A ball travelling

**TABLE 8.3** Misconceptions about forces

| |
| --- |
| **Common misconception** Forces make things move. |
| **Usual age for misconception** All ages. |
| **The scientific explanation** Forces can change the way things move, making them speed up, slow down or change direction. |
| **Ways to address the misconception** Provide examples of things moving with minimal frictions, like ice skaters or outer space and discuss the forces acting on objects. Compare the effects of friction. |

along a flat horizontal surface should, according to scientific theory, continue to move at a constant speed and never slow down, unless a force acts on it to make it slow down. We are aware that balls do slow down 'naturally', so we often presume that the moving ball has some energy, which gradually it loses. A scientific explanation is that the ball slows down because a force, which we call friction, acts on it. The result of the force is to decelerate the ball. If there were not a resistance force, then the ball would continue to move at a constant speed in the same direction forever. So there is not just the problem of opposing forces, but also the problem of infinity – the ball moving forever. Actually, there are four effects of forces that children do experience – the fourth is that forces can cause a change in shape in an object.

## Suggested activities

Frost (2002: 33) suggests a traditional science task – making and testing cotton reel rollers and recording the results onto a spreadsheet. Wind up the elastic band to store the energy in it, then measure the distance it goes for the number of twists you put in. Is there a pattern? Is it obvious? Yes, but the rollers never go in a straight line and they always skid a bit when you turn them tight and the elastic bands break and the friction is hard to overcome – so it all takes a long time. It can work better with washing-up liquid squeezy bottles, which are less fiddly and easier to make run straight. These work especially well if you put a tread on them made from corrugated card so that they do not skid so much.

## Numbers and spreadsheets

One of the problems you may find with spreadsheets like Excel is how to cope with averages – how to make sense of a number like 15.66667 when you are only eight years old? You may find that a child-friendly spreadsheet program like *Textease* is an easier one for young children. Have a look at the resources available in the school to see if there are others, for example, *NumberMagic* from Research Machines Window Box.

## 8.3 Food and energy

Littledyke *et al.* (2000) provide plenty of information on this topic, particularly in Chapter Six on energy and fuels. Two of the questions they raise and discuss are 'Is there energy in food?' and 'Does energy get used up?' Some of the science is quite difficult even for adults to understand, so it is important to avoid teaching children too much that may lead them to form the wrong concepts, which are more difficult to change later. However, we need to recognise both the correct scientific concepts and the everyday language that children will use to inform their own understanding. Many adults would say that there is energy in food; many children would also think that since we eat food to give us energy, then the food must contain energy. But the scientific explanation would be that food contains chemical bonds, which break when a reaction with oxygen takes place and that this process releases energy that our bodies can use.

## Environmental ideas

These also need to be explored. Some people suggest that recycling is a good answer to the problems of our production of waste matter, like bottles and newspaper. Yet there are alternatives that are more environmentally friendly. The three mantras of 'reduce', 'reuse' and 'recycle' should be considered alongside the understanding that recycling can cause further environmental degradation, since it requires more energy to carry it out.

## Farming and fishing

These are two dimensions of a big idea, subjects of human effort and with environmental consequences. Cod and salmon farming are subjects of current controversy, with salmon farmers complaining that the price of fresh salmon is now too low, while cod is not yet farmed but natural supplies are diminishing rapidly, especially North Sea stocks. Humans have used farming techniques for centuries, yet they are always changing, so we now have GM foods as an important issue, as well as crops that are resistant to pests and pests that are resistant to pesticides. Such issues perhaps are best left to discussion with older rather than younger children, who may be aware of them from their reading or watching of news stories on TV or films. Woodford (2000) presented a map of the potential links between science and ICT in the theme of food and farming. She started with the QCA scheme of work for ICT and showed where science about food and farming could fit with it. Some examples from her grid (Woodford 2000: 23–24), with an extra column showing the links to energy ideas, are presented in Table 8.4.

## Grow your own food

Try devising a scheme of work involving outdoor areas and using big ideas from science like life cycles, germination, water, energy, photosynthesis, health etc. If there are patches of outdoors available, you might work with the children to design an

**TABLE 8.4** ICT linked to food and farming and energy

| ICT skill and software | Food and farming link | Energy link |
|---|---|---|
| Controlling a floor turtle | Use the Roamer to illustrate the journey of an aspect of food or farming and use large 'stations' drawn on sheets of paper and placed on the floor, e.g. the journey of an egg from farm to shop to home to cake. | Discuss with children and research the amounts of energy involved in each of the stages of the journey. Identify the types of energy and transformations at each stage and the potential environmental consequences. |
| Combining text and graphics | Design an 'exercise is good for you' poster. | Identify the ways in which we 'use' our energy when we take part in 'energetic' activities. |

environmentally friendly growing area. Large plants like runner beans could be grown to demonstrate the cycles of life, from the germination of the seeds, through the stages of growth and development, to the growth of new flowers and eventual reproduction, perhaps with the help of pollinating insects and the production of new seeds. The outdoor area could be planted with species that attract insects and other minibeasts. Rotting logs and wood provide good cover for creatures like woodlice and worms. Compost areas can encourage detritivores and hedgehogs. Bird feeding tables can help children identify the species and numbers of visiting birds and see if these are dependent on seasons. If the outdoor area had areas of light and shade, ICT tools such as sensors and data-logging kits can be used to help measure and record environmental factors like temperature and amount of light.

## Wasting food

Is it possible to waste food in the sense that if humans do not eat the food then it is wasted? This argument is 'anthropocentric'. If we do not consume food materials, and the food then rots, it is likely that other organisms are eating it, even if these are microorganisms like bacteria or fungi. So food for humans then becomes food for other living organisms. So food, like energy, needs to be thought about in different ways.

## 8.4  Living things and the concept of 'alive'

## What is alive?

This is a good question to explore with children; one that raises all sorts of interesting misconceptions. There are seven major life processes common to humans and other animals, some of which should be taught to children in Key Stage 2, including nutrition, movement, growth and reproduction (DfEE 1999: 85). But even in Key Stage 1, children are to be taught about the difference between things that are living and things that have never been alive, and that animals, including humans, move, feed, grow, use their senses and reproduce. All these ideas involve the concept of energy.

## Compare yourself with a doll

An appropriate starting activity for younger children (maybe six-year-olds) would be looking at a doll and comparing what a doll cannot do with what they can do, or what a doll looks like with what they look like. You could use an interactive whiteboard to jot down some of the children's suggestions and comparisons. You should try to clarify the various meanings that children have of the word 'alive', through questions like:

- What is alive?

- What has never been alive?

- What was alive but is now dead?

- What was once part of a living thing, like a leaf or an apple that has fallen from a tree?

With older children, the questions could be more complex, such as:

- What about things like limestone, or other rocks, which were once the bones or shells of living things, but no longer have the form, shape, size or functions of these once living things?

## Helping children develop their ideas

Children's ideas can be sorted into definite stages, perhaps related to maturity or to prior experiences. Some young children equate living with having a face, or eyes especially. As they get older, they may change their criteria for life and suggest that movement is the main living feature. Harlen's view (2000) is that children learn by putting together a number of ideas into a larger framework or overarching concept. (How do children know that there are varieties of animals with four legs and a tail either called

**TABLE 8.5** Misconceptions about 'alive'

| |
|---|
| **Common misconceptions** The sun is alive because it moves. A car is alive because it moves. The moon is alive because people draw pictures of the man in the moon. |
| **Usual age for misconception** 5–8 years. |
| **The scientific explanation** Things are classified as alive if they exhibit the seven life processes: movement, respiration, sensitivity, growth, reproduction, excretion and nutrition. |
| **Ways to address the misconception** Ask children to say why they think things are alive. Ask them to compare a variety of pictures or real objects, animals and plants and sort them into alive or never been alive. Be prepared to wait for them to mature before they are ready for scientific explanations of alive. |

cats or dogs? By seeing, touching, stroking or otherwise interacting with a series of animals and adding them to their set of cat or dog. The concept of dog then undergoes transformation as it widens to include new types, shapes, sizes of dog.) There are a number of databases that will help children organise their thoughts about concepts concerning living things, especially branching key databases such as *Sorting Game* for BBC Acorn machines or *Flexitree* for PCs.

## Summary

In this chapter, you saw how the big idea of energy could be studied with children in a variety of contexts, such as the role of heat or light in germinating seeds, force and movement using toy cars, the energy contained in foods and the concepts of being alive.

You should now be able to:

- Plan lessons about the growth of plants that include a look at energy and the use of ICT tools.

- Understand how role play can help children learn about abstract concepts like electricity flow.

- Harness toys in the study of scientific concepts about forces and movement.

- Use the Internet to help with a study of energy values of foods.

- Plan a lesson to address the concept of being alive.

## Web links

http://www.ask.co.uk
Search engine Ask Jeeves.

http://www.ajkids.com/
Children's version of search engine.

# 'What if a chair was made of chocolate?' Materials and particles

## Introduction

This chapter deals with the big idea of the existence of particles as well as the **kinetic theory** of **matter**, but at a fairly basic level. Starting points about the science of materials in the primary school can range from stories like the Three Little Pigs through collections and observations of materials to investigations and testing of materials. The three pigs story does not often lead to investigations, but there are other stories that can. One of my favourites is Hansel and Gretel, with the Gingerbread House used by the wicked witch to entice the children in. This idea of a house made of gingerbread is the reason for the title of the chapter – a 'What if …' question that is dealt with in section 9.1. The following sections explore ideas about water in its three forms as solid, liquid and gas; then about materials dissolving in water; and finally about materials as thermal insulators.

## Learning objectives

By the end of the chapter, you should be able to plan and carry out activities concerning:

- Properties and function of materials – using Word and PowerPoint.
- Freezing, melting and condensation – using digital thermometers and the Internet.
- Dissolving and separating – using a digital microscope, spreadsheet and word processing.
- Insulating materials – using data logging, a digital thermometer and digital camera.

**TABLE 9.1    ICT National Curriculum links**

|  | Key Stage 1 (ages 5–7) | Key Stage 2 (ages 8–11) |
|---|---|---|
| Materials, properties and functions | 1a, 2a, 2d, 3a, 3b, 5b | 1a, 1b, 4b, 5a |
| Water and changes of state | 1a, 2b, 3a | 1a, 1c, 2a, 4a, 5a, 5b |
| Dissolving and separating | 1a, 1b, 1c | 4b |
| Insulation and heat | 1a, 3a, 5c | 2b, 3b |

**TABLE 9.2    QCA scheme links**

|  | Science | ICT |
|---|---|---|
| Materials, properties and functions | 1C, 3C, 5D | 1B, 3A, 6A |
| Water and changes of state | 2D, 3C, 5D | 2C, 6D |
| Dissolving and separating | 4D, 6C | 1D, 3C, 5D |
| Insulation and heat | 4C, 5D | 5E, 5F |

## Why is materials a big idea in science?

Materials is a big idea because it underpins the scientific explanation of the behaviour of matter. Materials and their properties constitute one of the four Attainment Targets in the National Curriculum. In Key Stage 1, for children aged five to seven years, this means studying how materials are grouped and classified and how materials can change through the application of forces and through heating and cooling. As children proceed into Key Stage 2 (aged eight to 11 years), they learn about more advanced classifications of materials, reversible and irreversible changes and separations of mixtures of materials. They do not have to understand about '**atoms**' and '**molecules**' yet, but teachers do have to lay the foundations for these more complex ideas. ICT can provide a context for these sorts of systems, which cannot be directly observed but can be modelled and simulated. Try looking for simulations of the water cycle using search engines for children, like Ask Jeeves Kids (http://www.ajkids.co.uk). Does your school have CD-ROMs that provide simulations of the properties of materials?

## Kinetic theory of matter

This theory simply stated is about the concept that all matter is made of atoms and molecules that move around constantly in different ways, depending on whether the matter is solid, liquid or gas. It also states that the temperature of matter is an indication of how fast the particles (or subatomic bits of particles) are moving. Look up this theory in one of the many books that deal with scientific theories (e.g. the Letts guides by Peacock 1998, 1999 or Wenham 1995 or a textbook at GCSE level or its equivalent). An alternative way to find out more is to search for the Kinetic Theory on a simple search engine such as Ask Jeeves. You will find a multiplicity of websites on the science background, some of which will provide simulations and diagrams, others giving more language-based explanations and still others giving you mathematical background too.

## Making the imperceptible perceptible

One of the main problems in dealing with materials and their properties was explored by the SPACE project team in schools in London and Liverpool, 'Making the imperceptible perceptible' (Osborne, Wadsworth, Black and Meadows 1994): making things bigger, so they can be more easily seen; making actions slower, so we can see them more easily, for example, through slow-motion photography; or faster, through time-lapse photos, so we can recognise the patterns in the phenomena. Matter at the level of our sensory perceptions behaves very differently from the way that science sees it behaving at a molecular or atomic level. There are Internet sites that provide simulations of complex ideas related to the behaviour of materials; see for example Ask Jeeves (www.ask.co.uk). Try another adult search engine, such as Lycos (www.lycos.com), but teachers need to be wary of making too much use of these American search engines. An alternative to all the US sites provided by some search engines is to use the UK version, such as www.lycos.co.uk.

## 9.1  Materials, properties and functions

### Lesson on materials

This section arose from observing a lesson on materials and their properties, planned and carried out by a final practice student in a Year 2 class in a school in a leafy suburb of London. The building was modern, ground floor only; the classroom was large and well resourced, opening inwards into a resource area/corridor and outwards to a paved area next to shrubs and grass, well away from main roads. The children had already had one lesson on sorting materials and were organised into groups based roughly on their English language abilities. During the group work period of the lesson, a higher ability group (although English language ability is a contested term and does not necessarily coincide with any scientific or ICT skills) discussed their ideas.

### Questions and discussions

Various questions and responses arose from them and from their teacher, such as:

> 'What are paving stones made of? Maybe they are cement? Or concrete, or rock, or stone?'
> 'How can we find out? How do we know? We've seen them before. They look like stone.'

**TABLE 9.3** Pupil resource: Materials and their properties

| Name | Date | |
|---|---|---|
| What are you looking at? | What do you think it is made of? | Why do you think so? |
| A door frame | Wood | Because it sounds like wood when you bang it |
| | | |
| | | |
| | | |

Then, as the grass had been cut that morning, one child asked:

'What is grass made of?'

She asked an adult who might know the answer and might help her to fill in the worksheet (see Table 9.3 for the worksheet). The adult could not deal with the question, so like a 'good teacher' deflected it by asking, 'What do you think it's made of?' then 'Where does it grow?' The answer, 'It grows in the soil', then led to asking 'What is soil made of … how do we know … feel it … look at it etc.' During the plenary section, further questioning and sharing of children's ideas took place and the 'what if …' ideas began.

Fill in the table – the first part is done as an example.

# A 'What if' book

The lesson about materials could then continue into another, exploring the alternatives to real materials. For example, make a multi-section book, from card and spiral binding, or a multimedia ICT-based book that has a variety of types of object and a number of different types of materials, linked by the phrases 'what if … was made of …?'

Use Word and clip art (or PowerPoint) to organise the pages in your book with text and pictures. Take the words 'chair' and 'chocolate' as your starting object and material, and then replace the object by words such as 'window', 'cake', 'book', 'oven'. Then replace the material type with words such as 'paper', 'stone', 'glass', 'metal'. This type of question (see Chapter 12 for further examples of questioning) can be classified as 'thought experiments', although some can lead to actual investigations and searches for information. Some may lead to surprising discoveries even for adults, especially in our technologically developed society, where many materials have a wide variety of uses and functions. Some good examples of 'What if' books already exist and are widely used in primary schools:

*Ketchup on Your Cornflakes* (1994) by Nick Sharratt, a two-section spiral-bound book;

*Fish Go Woof* (2003) by Miranda Maxwell-Hyslop, a three-section spiral-bound book.

## Developing children's ideas

What sort of responses would you expect from children to these sorts of 'What if' questions? What further action should you take when faced with these responses? Perhaps looking closely at different objects in the environment and analysing the materials they were made of would be a useful start? If the response was 'It would melt if I sat on it', what then? You might ask further questions about what other materials would also melt, such as butter or margarine? If the response was 'Someone might eat the legs off and it would fall over', what then? You could raise questions about how many legs does a chair need to still stand up? How about a question like, 'What if an oven was made of glass?' Part of an oven could easily be made of this material and often the door of an oven is made of specially strengthened glass.

## Creative thinking

The idea of the 'What if' book is not just to point out that materials have specific functions, but also to provoke creative thinking – helping children to realise that learning science can be fun sometimes and is not just about learning facts. Part of the reason for such books is to promote the idea that alternative ideas can be discussed in non-threatening ways and that there is not always one right answer; that a teacher does not always have the right answer and that real science is about finding out unknown answers.

## 9.2  Water and changes of state

### Evaporation and condensation

Ideas and concepts about particles can be approached through evaporation and condensation, where invisible particles of water from the air appear on cold surfaces in damp places, steam on windows in bathroom or kitchen, breath in the air on frosty days. States of matter experiments can be fun to do with children and should be linked to questions like, 'Is water still the same thing when it is frozen as ice?' (There are three states of matter: solid, liquid and gas.) Even if children are not yet ready in the primary school for abstract concepts about kinetic theory and molecules of water at different temperatures, teachers need to be aware of the demands and requirements of the next stage in children's school learning (QTT standard 2.3). We need to provide appropriate experiences and ideas that children can build on.

Trying to deal with the second misconception in Table 9.4 is not easy – some students worked with children aged between eight and nine years on this problem and found that even when they did put coloured water or coloured ice cubes inside the cans but the condensation was not coloured, the children still found other ways to explain the concept they hold. In this case, one child said that the colour stays inside the tin and only the water gets out.

**TABLE 9.4** Misconceptions about heat and cold

| |
| --- |
| **Common misconception 1** There are two types of electricity: one is hot and makes heaters work, the other is cold and makes fridges and freezers work. |
| **Usual age for misconception** 5–6 years. |
| **The scientific explanation** Electricity is not hot or cold, but it can make hot or cold effects. |
| **Ways to address the misconception** Ask other children in the class what they think about the idea? Try a thought experiment: would the fridge work if you plugged it into a different socket? |
| **Common misconception 2** Condensation forms on the outside of a tin containing a mixture of ice and water – this water comes leaking out of the tin itself. |
| **Usual age for misconception** 8–10 years. |
| **The scientific explanation** Condensation is caused by water vapour in the air. As the air cools, the water vapour condenses onto the cold surface. |
| **Ways to address the misconception** Try adding coloured water to the can or container and ask the children to predict whether the condensation will now be coloured. |

## Iceberg models

Make a model iceberg by filling a balloon with cold water and putting it into the freezer. With the model iceberg, children can explore rates and patterns of melting, changes in temperature of the surrounding water and think about the particles of water as they change from solid to liquid. Try using dye in the frozen balloons, so children can observe the water from the iceberg as it mixes with warmer water in a tank. A transparent tank, made of plastic, is most suitable for this (not a glass fish tank or a washing-up bowl). The changes in temperature can be measured with a digital thermometer or even better by linking the thermometer to a computer in order to produce a graph of the changes in temperature against time. More ideas about exploring children's ideas through ice balloon activities can be found in Harlen (2000) and in *Primary Science Review* (Ovens 1987). Harlen raises some 'What would happen if' questions about the ice balloons, aimed at gathering evidence about their ideas:

What if you put ink on the ice?

What if you put salt on it?

What if you poke it?

She also suggests using concept maps and children's writing to collect further evidence.

## Supporting slower writers with ICT

Both these methods can be supported through the use of ICT – *Illuminatus* is a concept mapping program, for example, although *Clicker* and other word banks will also help children to construct similar concept maps and *My World* sentence programs allow children or teachers to write beginnings, middles and ends of sentences and rearrange these flexibly.

## The concept of humidity

Although children may find it relatively simple to associate the bits of ice with bits of water, it is often much harder for them to recognise that water as a gas is also composed of particles – individual bits of matter moving in the air as water vapour. The concept of humidity can be experienced, perhaps during a visit to Kew Gardens or another greenhouse, maybe in a local garden centre. Humidity sensors are also available if you want to use ICT to make the measuring more accurate. It is important that children experience the concept of humidity as well as just measuring it. Some children may be able to link this to their travels in more humid climates. This should provide the stimulus for discussion and the raising of questions, leading to further investigations such as drying clothes in different conditions: inside a warm damp room; inside a room with a hair drier; outdoors in the wind; outdoors in a sunny spot.

## 9.3 Dissolving and separation of materials

### Some questions

Can you see really small particles?

What is the smallest size of particle you can actually see?

What happens to tiny grains of salt, for example, when you put them into water?

These sorts of questions can be used to start off a discussion about particles in order to find out what ideas and concepts children already hold.

Tiny dust particles in the air can be seen in strong sunlight, especially if the sunlight enters a room through a small gap. Another way of helping children to see tiny particles is to set up a clear plastic tank of water in a dark room, sprinkle some talcum powder into the water, then shine a powerful torch through the tank.

### Magnifiers

We can help children to see small particles more clearly through magnifying them – the obvious progression would be using your eye, then a magnifying glass, then a microscope. But be aware of the difficulties that children may have when they first start using these tools – they may think that what they see is not the same thing when they use a microscope. The best microscopes are binocular ones, which are heavy enough not to wobble and which have an inbuilt light. Crystals of sugar and salt are useful to look at through these.

**TABLE 9.5** Misconceptions about dissolving

| |
|---|
| **Common misconception** When something dissolves, it is no longer there at all. |
| **Usual age for misconception** Key Stage 1, but some also in Key Stage 2. |
| **The scientific explanation** There is some controversy about the scientific explanations for dissolving, but it is certain that the original material is still there in some form in the solution, although it may exist in an ionised state, rather than as whole molecules. |
| **Ways to address the misconception** Try using taste tests to see if the substance can be detected when compared to pure water. (You have to ensure that safe conditions apply for testing with taste.) |

## Microscopes

A digital microscope can be a useful tool to support activities about dissolving and separating. Fairly cheap microscopes are now available in primary schools, which can be hand held or mounted in a stand and linked to the USB port of most computers. They can also be linked to projectors so that the whole class can see the magnified images. Try setting up such a microscope to look at crystals such as salt and sugar. Different types of sugar make interesting comparisons; try Demerara or castor sugar, for example. Simple experiments can be carried out with dissolving sugar or salt in water, measuring the amount that is put in, then allowing the water to evaporate (over a weekend perhaps would be sensible, to prevent children interfering with the experimental set-up). Then look at the crystals again under the microscope to see whether they appeared to be in the same form as the original crystals.

## Spreadsheets and dissolving sugars

A spreadsheet could be used to support investigations into the speed of dissolving of sugar – then make a bar graph to compare the results from different sugars. The children should be encouraged to examine the size of the various particles and perhaps make some predictions. Do they think that the larger the particles, the slower they will dissolve? Other variables to consider might include whether the solution was stirred, and how often, or the size of the container, or the amount of water used. A prediction chart made using Word and perhaps with word banks, might be helpful for some children who are less motivated or less able in writing English.

## Does the solute just disappear?

The solute is the stuff that dissolves in the liquid. But icing sugar will not work for this, because you can go on adding it to water indefinitely – it just creates a thicker and thicker paste and does not really dissolve at all. Salt, on the other hand, works much better, but it is hard to see when it has all dissolved. One of the easiest things to use is a sugar lump, since this can be seen most clearly. The interesting misconception that often occurs here is that because the sugar disappears, it is no longer there at all. How could this be explored? Well, tasting the mixture should provide the answer – children will taste that the water is sweet or salty, so challenge them to produce explanations for that fact.

## What's in a tin of beans?

One useful context for teaching about dissolving is that of food. You might collect a variety of baked bean cans, again with help from the children. Examine the lists of ingredients to see what else is included, especially whether there is salt and sugar added to the sauce. A database can then be set up showing the varieties and the amounts of each substance dissolved. Children could then use their scientific skills to interpret this data and draw conclusions about the more or less healthy brands of baked beans. Since most ingredient lists identify the weight of the substance per 100 grams, a spreadsheet would be a useful tool for converting the amounts into various other ratios. Some children (differentiation would be important in planning this sort of activity) might be able to extend the spreadsheet activities to include health aspects, if they were helped to gain access to figures concerning what children and adults should be eating. (See also Chapter 5 on living things and Chapter 8 on food and energy.)

## Taste testing

Another context could be taste tests. (Anything children eat or drink should be subject to advice about allergies.) Children could be encouraged to make a variety of different concentrations of sugar in water and then test their solutions on other groups to see whether they could put the different solutions in order. Word and clip art could then be used to make records of the investigations and perhaps identify who has the most sensitive sense of taste. A variation of this could be diluting orange or blackcurrant drinks with different amounts of water and comparing taste with colour.

## Warmer or colder dissolving

Further contexts could be about how fast things dissolve in cold, tepid or warm water. The QCA scheme for science (6C) suggests an activity with the context of a manufacturer of artificial sweeteners, who needs to know how long it takes for the sweetener to dissolve in chilled water, water at room temperature or warm/hot water. It also suggests some complex analysis of the results, using overhead transparencies of several graphs. ICT tools would be much more useful for this kind of comparison, since several different graphs can be displayed on screen at the same time. These graphs can then be displayed in modern classrooms, using interactive whiteboards.

## Predictions and word processing

Another context suggested in the QCA scheme is to draw together 'work' in the unit with a series of cards making predictions, such as, 'I think when you evaporate sweetened tea the sugar will evaporate with the water.' In this instance, ICT could again be a useful tool to support the learning of science, since the predictions could be typed by children into a word processor and saved for use at different times and by other classes. They could be used as alternative ideas for children to agree or disagree with and to help them to set up investigations to test out their predictions.

## 9.4 Insulation and heat

Insulating and conducting properties of materials need to be investigated, as they lead eventually to more concepts about particle theories.

### Keeping the tea warm?

One common investigation about thermal conductivity you may see in books on primary science involves various cups of hot liquids; one common context for doing this experiment is keeping the teacher's cup of tea warm. This can be linked to monitoring of the temperature of the tea through a digital thermometer and an interface with a computer, so that a graph is drawn automatically. Feasey and Gallear (2001) suggest doing experiments with Key Stage 1 children about measuring the temperatures of four cups of water which contain ice water, cold water, warm water and hot (but not boiling) water. They also suggest using digital thermometers to measure the temperatures.

### Problems with hot experiments

What is not clear is how children themselves would be involved in thinking about and doing most of this type of work, since there are dangers in having hot liquids in the classroom and even more concerns about liquids near expensive computers. Another problem is that experiments with cooling of hot liquids rarely give good results because of the number of variables. A particular problem is that heat can be transferred through the top and bottom of a container as well as through the sides; another is that taking the temperature affects the results.

### Hot and cold in everyday life

Could you and the children you are working with be a little more creative and imaginative in finding a context for investigations of hot things? Try brainstorming ideas with a group of children about investigations related to their own experiences – how can you keep your hands warm when it is cold outside? What sort of glove is best to keep out the wet when you are throwing snowballs? What sort of glove is best for keeping out the cold wind? What if gloves were made of glass? You could use digital thermometers to measure the temperatures of hands and of the outside environment. Try using stories as contexts for investigations about hot and cold. What if a mountain climber in the Alps wanted to melt some ice for a drink? How should she do it quickly? If she wrapped it in her glove? Or in some cotton wool? Or held it in her hands?

**TABLE 9.6** Misconceptions about insulation

| |
|---|
| **Common misconception** Silver foil helps to keep things cool or warm. |
| **Usual age for misconception** Key Stage 1, but some may continue to think this until much later in life. |
| **The scientific explanation** Silver foil is really aluminium and is a good conductor of heat, so it will not keep things any hotter or colder than their environment. |
| **Ways to address the misconception** Try the classic investigation of wrapping things in different materials – but use ice cubes rather than hot water in containers – and see which one melts more quickly. |

We use foil in the oven to wrap chicken or fish during cooking – so it must allow heat through or the food would not cook. This misconception concerns the fact that heat can be transferred in three ways: conduction, convection and radiation. Foil is a good reflector of radiant heat, but a good conductor of heat too.

## Summary

In this chapter, you have read about the difficulties of exploring particles directly in the primary classroom, but have seen how to help children use ICT tools to think more deeply about materials and their properties. You explored ideas about freezing and melting water, about dissolving and about heat insulation.

You should now be able to:

- Carry out a creative activity, making a 'What if' book, to help children think about the properties of materials.
- Plan and carry out lessons on freezing and melting of water and solutions, taking children's misconceptions into account.
- Recognise a range of activities about dissolving of materials and use ICT tools to support these.
- Explore heat insulation through a range of relevant investigations.

## Web links

http://www.ask.co.uk
To search for background knowledge and simulations about the Kinetic Theory.

http://www.ajkids.com/
This is the children's version.

www.lycos.co.uk
Search engine UK version.

www.lycos.com
The US version.

http://www.epa.gov/region07/kids/wtrcycle.htm
A US site giving information about the water cycle.

www.teachtsp.com
Another US site that gives some hands-on activities about the water cycle.

http://www.bbc.co.uk/cbeebies/tweenies/
A BBC site about popular TV characters, the Tweenies.

# 10

# Cells: 'What is grass made of?'

## Introduction

This chapter introduces the idea of a cell as the building block upon which life on earth is constructed. It suggests a variety of activities that teachers can carry out with children which will lead to them being able to understand the concept of a cell in their later scientific education, without actually dealing with this concept in their primary school education in any formal way. One section of the chapter arises from investigations carried out by a student teacher with children aged seven and eight years, exploring what things are made from and then looking at plants more closely. The other sections deal with aspects of the human body and its organs. One question raised is, 'What happens to the food inside your body?' and what children might expect to understand about the processes involved in digestion. Our skin contains cells of many types and the third section of this chapter looks at two of these – touch and taste cells – and the associate senses. Finally, we look at the heart and circulation of the blood, since the cells that make up our blood are essential for vital life processes, especially respiration.

## Learning objectives

By the end of this chapter you should be able to:

■ Plan some activities that will help children, later in their lives, to make sense of the concept of a living cell, by investigating materials, raising questions and developing ideas about plants – using light meters and spreadsheets.

■ Identify children's ideas about what is inside them and how they digest food, helping them to develop these into more scientific explanations – using CD-ROMs and ICT-based drawing packages.

■ Plan activities about sense cells, especially touch, taste and smell – using the Internet, spreadsheets and CD-ROMs.

■ Support children learning about blood, heart and heart beat, and the role of blood in regulating body temperature – using pulse meters and digital thermometers, CD-ROMs and databases.

**TABLE 10.1   ICT National Curriculum links**

|  | Key Stage 1 (ages 5–7) | Key Stage 2 (ages 8–11) |
|---|---|---|
| Plants and photosynthesis | 1b, 5b | 2b, 5b, 5c |
| Food inside you | 1a, 1d, 2b | 1a, 1b, 5b |
| Touch and taste | 1a, 1b, 3b | 1a, 1b, 2c |
| Heart and blood | 1a, 1b, 5b | 1a, 1b, 1c, 2b, 2c |

**TABLE 10.2   QCA scheme links**

|  | Science | ICT |
|---|---|---|
| Plants and photosynthesis | 1B, 2B, 3B, 5B | 1B, 2B, 6B |
| Food inside you | 1A, 2A, 3A, 5A | 1C, 2B, 3A |
| Touch and taste | 1A, 2A, 3A, 5A | 1D, 5B, 5D, 6D |
| Heart and blood | 1A, 2A, 4A, 5A | 1A, 2D, 3C |

## Why is the cell a big idea?

Cells are one of the major themes in Key Stage 3 science in the National Curriculum for England and Wales (DfEE 1999). However, cells are also too small to see with the naked eye, so they are not easy for young children to recognise. Similarly the concept of a cell as the basic building block of plants and animals is not an easy one to understand. Cell division is the process that enables the growth of plants and animals as well as reproduction. There is a big difference between plant and animal cells which determines their very different functions as producers and consumers. Yet there are also many similarities between the plant and animal cells, such as the possession of a cell membrane to cover the cell; a nucleus that contains information and controls the activities of the cell; and cytoplasm where chemical reactions take place.

What we will mostly be concerned with in this chapter is the similarities and differences between cells when they are grouped together in sufficiently large collections for young children to study them.

## 10.1  Grass and plants, investigating photosynthesis

### Exploring materials

A group of children were exploring the materials in their environment outside the class-room, trying to use their experience and as many of their senses as possible to work out what things are made from. They looked at paving stones and touched and tapped them to check that they were hard and did not sound like wood or feel like metal. So they were using at least three senses to explore the materials: vision, hearing and touch. Another sense then came into play, as the grass in the surrounding area had been recently cut and they could smell it.

### Raising questions and finding answers

One of the questions that arose was, 'What is grass made of?' How could a teacher help children to find an answer to this question?

You could point them to a book or an Internet site, show them a video or tell them that grass is a plant and is made of cells. But would any of this help these seven- and eight-year-olds to understand, rather than to merely repeat the information? Would looking closely at grass or other plants help children to understand what grass is made of? Probably not, so what would be reasonable activities for a teacher to plan to help children make some progress with answering their question?

### Can you always find answers?

Have a look at Chapter 8 section 8.4 for ideas that explore concept of being alive. Is grass alive? Has the cut grass ever been alive? How do we know if it is alive or not? We then help children come to criteria for classifying grass or other plants as being alive, such as does it move? Does it grow? Does it breathe? Does it eat? Can it feel things, like the warmth of the sun? This is, of course, linked to the seven life processes, most of which we need to teach to children in the primary school. But there are some questions that we cannot answer completely in the primary school and this is one of them.

### Developing ideas about plants

When helping children to develop their ideas about plants, as opposed to animals, we need to explore three main areas: the parts of flowering plants, the functions of parts of a plant and the stages in reproduction of flowering plants. The key ideas are that plants are one group of living things and can be flowering or non-flowering; that they need light, water, carbon dioxide and oxygen and nutrients to grow; and that plants can make food from water and carbon dioxide in the presence of light and chlorophyll – this process is called photosynthesis (SPACE 1995c: 79).

## An experiment to avoid

There is a common experiment about plant stems which you may see in some books about science experiments for young children. It suggests taking cut flowers, especially white flowers, and standing them in coloured water so that children can see that the colour in the water rises up the stems and changes the colour of the flowers. Carnations are often suggested for this experiment or, as an alternative, celery sticks. The science behind this is to do with capillary action and plant cells. But this experiment does not often answer questions raised by the children; neither does it lead to an increase in young children's understanding of cells.

## Experiments or investigations?

Children may enjoy these kinds of experiments; they may raise useful discussion, but because they fail to relate to children's own ideas and questions, they may also give rise to misconceptions and to seeing science as just repeating experiments that others have done and to which the teacher already knows the answer. One of the biggest ideas in science is that we do science because we do not know the answer to a question, not because we are 'required to prove' something.

**TABLE 10.3** Misconceptions about plants

| |
|---|
| **Common misconception 1** Plants need food and they get it from the soil. |
| **Usual age for misconception** Key Stage 1, but some may continue to think this until much later in life. |
| **The scientific explanation** Plants make 'food' from the energy of the sun and from carbon dioxide and water. |
| **Ways to address the misconception** Try growing cuttings of plants in just water, without soil, or grow cress seeds on cotton wool, instead of soil. Do they grow without soil? |
| **Common misconception 2** Plants are not alive because they do not move, they do not look like people, they do not have a face etc. |
| **Usual age for misconception** Key Stage 1 usually. Most children develop more sophisticated ideas about living things during Key Stage 2. |
| **The scientific explanation** Plants are alive because they respire, reproduce, grow, move, are sensitive, excrete and need nutrition. |
| **Ways to address the misconception** Ask questions like, 'Can plants die?' If they can, they must be alive. Ask other questions like, 'Do they grow?', or 'Do some of them move?' Focus on the seven aspects of living things. |

## How can we develop a creative approach to photosynthesis?

A creative approach to photosynthesis and other aspects of plant growth needs to challenge children themselves to come up with relevant questions and then to help them to find answers to these questions. For example, plants need light to grow – everyone knows this, but how much light is necessary and how can we find the best conditions? How can we separate light from heat? How can we help children set up investigations to explore quantitatively the amount of light and the effect of this light on plant growth? In this activity, no one would really know the exact answer to the questions posed, because every situation in a primary school will be slightly different. You could help the children to prepare some small growing plants, either by planting some suitable seeds and letting them germinate or by buying plants already growing in small pots. Then place the plants in a variety of different settings, while measuring the light intensity in each one. This activity needs to take place over a week or two, in order to see any results. Measuring the light intensity also needs to take place several times a day and then an average taken. But making it relevant to children's ideas would need good preparation and recognition of their current thinking and suggestions. So a creative teacher would take the suggested ideas and change them to suit the circumstances of their class or group.

## 10.2 Digestion – what happens to the food inside you?

### Research about children's ideas

Research from the SPACE project (1995c: 59–64) reveals that children display some fascinating ideas about the insides of their bodies and what happens to food. Some think that food goes into the different bits of our bodies; if you ask them to draw what happens to the food, they may show bits of bread and sausages floating around inside their arms and legs. Older children also show some interesting misconceptions about where the food goes. Obviously in a primary school, we cannot investigate practically what does happen, so it may seem that the only way to deal with this aspect of the curriculum is through passive learning techniques. But this is not necessary at all. A good starting point, as usual in science teaching, is to find out what children already think and then base your teaching on these ideas. But with such a variety of ideas already available from the research, teachers do not start with a blank slate. Teachers can probably assume that some children will display a few of the ideas and so make some plans in advance of the lesson, which will address these misconceptions. Children could use ICT-based drawing programs to prepare their pictures.

### Children's ideas about digestion

To make this a more creative teaching process, ask children why they think certain things about digestion. This will help them to understand their own thinking and make

**TABLE 10.4** Common misconceptions about food

| |
|---|
| **Common misconception1** The food we eat goes to all parts of our bodies. |
| **Usual age for misconception** Younger children, aged five and six. |
| **The scientific explanation** The food is broken down in your mouth, stomach and small intestine. The smaller molecules are absorbed into the blood vessels in small and large intestines and then transported around the body. |
| **Ways to address the misconception** Give the children a plain water biscuit to eat and ask them to keep it in their mouth for as long as possible. Ask them to describe what it feels like just before they swallow. Try this with other foods that are partly digested by the saliva in your mouth. |
| **Common misconception2** The solids go down one tube in your throat, the liquids go down another tube. |
| **Usual age for misconception** Key Stage 1 and and early part of Key Stage 2 for some children. |
| **The scientific explanation** Solids and liquids go down the same tube to your stomach, but gases go down and up a different tube in your throat. |
| **Ways to address the misconception** This is not an easy one to address practically. Children could look inside each others' mouths as well as looking at CD-ROMs showing the inside of the body. |

them more open to changing their ideas than if they are just told or shown current scientific ideas. One eight-year-old said that he thought there were two tubes inside your throat, one for the solid food and one for the liquids. When asked why, he told us that since the food eventually comes out through two different places, then it must get separated in the first place into these two different types. So he was reconciling what he knew, that there are two tubes inside your throat (although one is for gases, not for liquids), with what he thought was sensible. The teaching that he needed would then focus on eating and drinking and focusing on how it felt. Perhaps the children could eat plain water biscuits slowly and explain to each other what they felt happening in their mouths (bearing in mind that anything children eat or drink should be subject to advice about allergies). Does it feel as if the biscuit, mixed with saliva, goes down one tube or two? Helping children to make a three-dimensional model of the digestive system would be a useful way to support their learning.

## 10.3 Magnifying your skin – touch and taste cells

### Which cells can we investigate easily?

All of our body is made up of cells, some of them specialised and organised into organs like the lungs and brain. But most of our cells are too difficult to investigate in the primary school, except for some of the ones on the outer parts of our bodies. Sensitive cells exist in our skin to help us recognise objects and temperatures, smells and tastes. These cells are relatively easy to investigate, although children will often be unaware that it is really cells that we are dealing with.

## Investigating touch with a feely bag

Children of all ages can be encouraged to explore their touch sense, often by blindfolding them or by putting objects out of sight inside a box or feely bag. Feely bag or box collections are common in nursery classes and Key Stage 1. You just need a collection of familiar objects inside a bag or box and then encourage the children to feel them without looking. They could respond in a number of ways; for example, by just guessing what the objects are, or by trying to describe the object to someone else without telling them what they think it is. A pair of identical objects could be used, with one inside the bag and the other outside, so that children can compare their visual with touch senses and try to match the one they touch with the one they see.

## Touch tests

If you want to investigate touch with older children, try a variation of this one, using corks and dressmaking pins. Stick one or two pins into a cork, put the children into groups of about four, blindfold one of them and get the others to devise a test to tell whether the blindfolded child can identify a single or double pin touch on different parts of their hand. The main purpose, besides investigating the presence of touch-sensitive cells in our skin, is for children to devise their own systems for recording results and then interpreting them. The science behind this is that we can feel when there are two pins, if we have two touch-sensitive cells close enough together in that patch of skin. A spreadsheet could be used to help children record the results of this investigation.

## Taste and smell

There are four types of taste-sensing cells on your tongue. Look these up in a primary science book or use an ICT source. Rather than doing experiments to prove this existing knowledge, try to disprove it, using children's own ideas and simple equipment like cotton buds and salt and sugar solutions. While we can only identify four tastes with our tongues, we often say we can taste many other things. What really happens is that the smell-sensitive cells in our noses are doing the tasting, which is why you sometimes lose your sense of 'taste' when you have a heavy cold. We can test this out by asking children to hold their noses while tasting a fruit-flavoured sweet. Can they identify the flavour without looking or smelling? What happens when they let go of their noses? Does the smell, rather than the sweet taste, now come through?

**TABLE 10.5** Misconceptions about taste

| |
|---|
| **Common misconception** We can taste flavours like oranges or strawberries. |
| **Usual age for misconception** Key Stage 2 – younger children may have this, but would not be ready to deal with the distinction. |
| **The scientific explanation** We can only taste four things – sweet, sour, salt and bitter – because we only have four types of taste buds in our mouths. All our other tastes are really smells. |
| **Ways to address the misconception** Try tasting things with your nose blocked – pinch your nose and blind test a flavoured sweet like a fruit pastille. |

## Tasting salty crisps

Taste tests are explored in a book from Planet Science's Creative Classrooms (see www.planet-science.com) campaign: Which crisps are the saltiest? (Duncan and Bell 2002: 14). They suggest that you ask pupils to set up their own investigation of which of three types of crisps are the saltiest, in order to help their teacher choose the healthier brand, as he has high blood pressure and should be on a low salt diet. A more creative approach would be to ask the children themselves to set the context for an investigation, rather than using the ready-made adult context (bearing in mind advice about allergies). One suggestion provided is to use a microscope to try and count the grains of salt – for our purposes, this should be a digital microscope. An interesting idea from this publication is to provide the pupils with open-ended recording sheets to help them sort out their ideas, for example, 'Discuss the problem in your group and come up with five different ways for comparing the amount of salt in different crisps' (p.16).

## 10.4 Heart and circulation

## Pulse and breathing rates

Most children are aware that they have a heart and a pulse or heartbeat. They can easily feel their heart beating faster and are aware of their breathing getting faster (getting out of breath) when they do a lot of strenuous exercise. But they are likely to confuse the functions of lungs and heart, as the breathing and pulse rates seem similar to them. Although breathing rate seems to be easy to measure, it is actually affected by the measuring, since once you start to think about your breathing, you often consciously slow it down or speed it up. Pulse rate is less under our conscious control, but is much more difficult for young children to measure accurately. Probably the best way to do this is with a digital pulse meter, which just clips onto a child's thumb or a pulse-reading wristwatch. If you have not got either of these, then feeling for a pulse at wrist, chest or neck can be done with older children.

## Modelling the circulation

An interesting activity for children to carry out is to make models of the insides of their bodies in three dimensions. Drawings and two-dimensional representations of the insides of our bodies can be very confusing, since bodies are themselves three-dimensional. A good starting point would be to ask children to draw round one of their friends and then show where the heart would be, in comparison to other main organs like lungs, bones, brain, stomach and intestines. The next stage might be to compare these drawings with others from books, but a better idea is to use a CD-ROM like the *Amazing Human Body* (Dorling Kindersley), which lets children look at organs like the heart from a variety of directions. Ask children to draw the shape of their hearts and do not be surprised when they make the traditional Valentine shape. Making the model helps children to focus on functions rather than preconceived ideas about shape. Hence, if the heart is seen as functioning like a pump, then some kind of pump model will be needed for the model heart, such as a squeezy bottle, linked to tubes to carry the blood.

## Body temperatures

One of the functions of blood is to help maintain the temperature of different parts of our bodies. This is one area that children can explore using digital and other thermometers, though avoiding glass ones. Forehead thermometers that use LCD screen technology are now common – these give a reading that is easy to see and a colour change – much easier than the traditional glass thermometer and safer to use by children. Different parts of the body tend to have different temperatures with extremities like fingers and toes being cooler than more central parts, like armpits or mouth. But our bodies are also well regulated through blood flow, so the temperatures do not rise all that much when we exercise, if we allow our skin to help in the regulation. Try out some measurements of body temperatures with children who are exercising in well-ventilated places, so that they can experience the ways in which their bodies carry out this regulation role. With older children, this active investigation can be supplemented by second-hand study of different types of animal, especially the so-called

**TABLE 10.6** Misconceptions about blood

| |
|---|
| **Common misconception** Blood is everywhere in your body, since wherever you cut yourself, you bleed. |
| **Usual age for misconception** 5–8 years. |
| **The scientific explanation** Blood flows through blood vessels – arteries from the heart and veins to the heart – while tiny vessels called capillaries take blood to and from all the other organs. |
| **Ways to address the misconception** Look carefully at the veins near to your skin, for example in your arms, and feel the pulse in arteries near the skin, for example in your neck. |

cold-blooded reptiles. CD-ROMs and the Internet are useful resources in this type of secondary study. Looking at the ways in which some reptiles warm up their body and blood by basking in the sun can lead to investigations using temperature sensors, as suggested by Frost (2002: 121), where he asks the question 'Do astronauts keep cool in shiny suits?' He recommends making model astronauts and dressing some in foil and others in fabric; then using a desk lamp to shine on them as a substitute for the sun; then using temperature sensors to measure the increase in temperature inside the astronaut's spacesuit. Would children be able to link this to the reverse operation, when the 'cold' lizard tries to warm its body temperature by basking in the sun's rays? In both cases, the role of the blood and circulation is crucial in taking the heat around the body of lizard or astronaut.

## Summary

In this chapter, you have seen how creative ideas about growing plants will help children develop their ideas about living things; how children's own ideas about what is inside their bodies can be used to help them develop more scientific concepts; how to use data packages to support investigations into the senses, pulse rates and body temperature.

You should now be able to:

- Raise questions with children about plant growth and plan appropriate ways of answering these questions.
- Identify children's ideas about what is inside them and how they digest food, helping them to develop these into more scientific explanations.
- Plan activities about sense cells, especially touch, taste and smell.
- Support children's learning about blood, heart and pulse rate and the role of blood in regulating body temperature.

## Web link

www.planet-science.com
Planet Science started up as Science Year 2001, but has continued to inspire young people to learn about science – and enjoy it too.

# Learning out of school

## Introduction

This chapter explores the ways in which learning can take place out of the school. Taking children outside the classroom can provide them with learning contexts that enrich their experience of more formal school activities. It can also be a problem for inexperienced teachers and student teachers. The chapter gives some examples of interesting out-of-school teaching and learning in science and ICT, including children and student teachers learning in these contexts.

## Learning objectives

By the end of this chapter you will be able to:

■ Recognise the potential of learning out of school – using data-logging equipment and digital cameras.

■ Identify places in the built environment that can be used to support children's learning of scientific ideas and skills – using branching key databases.

■ Plan activities that link science and ICT learning with cross-curricular themes involving other subjects – using designing software.

■ Recognise the potential of the school grounds and other natural sites for teaching and learning with science and ICT – using spreadsheets and digital cameras.

**TABLE 11.1    ICT National Curriculum links**

|  | Key Stage 1 (ages 5–7) | Key Stage 2 (ages 8–11) |
|---|---|---|
| Public places | 1a, 1b, 5a, 5c | 1a, 1b, 2a, 2b, 5c |
| Buildings | 1b, 3a | 2b, 3b, 5a, 5c |
| The built environment | 1b, 1c, 2c, 5c | 2b, 5b, 5c |
| The natural environment | 1b, 3a, 5c | 2b, 2c, 3b, 5b |

**TABLE 11.2   QCA scheme links**

|  | Science | ICT |
|---|---|---|
| Public places | 2B, 5/6H | 2B, 3C, 6C |
| Buildings | 2F, 3C, 3D | 2E, 5D |
| The built environment | 2F, 5C, 5F | 3A, 3C, 4C, 6C |
| The natural environment | 2B, 4B | 2B, 3A, 5D |

## Why is learning out of school a big idea?

The *Excellence and Enjoyment* document (DfES 2003: 47–55) provides case studies of learning out of school hours. The notion of an extended school from the DfES is one that goes out into the community; uses volunteers from local businesses who read with children; invites in local firefighters who give talks and demonstrations; provides study support for out-of-school-hours learning including sport and outdoor activities, creative arts and clubs for ICT, maths and languages. The extended school teaches positive behaviour for all children, encouraging active citizenship ideas where children act as peer mentors or playground helpers. It supports the notion that an informal curriculum time exists just before school, during playtimes and lunchtimes: this is critical in behaviour improvement but also critical for ICT opportunities and incidental learning about and through the environment.

## Learning out of school in other chapters

In previous chapters, there have been examples of teaching and learning done outside the classroom:

- See Chapter 3 for a case study of children exploring animals and plants with three adults in the school grounds.

- See Chapter 5 for ideas about investigating minibeasts, bringing them into the classroom and returning them at the end of the lesson; for ideas about the topic of containers and packaging, ideas about growing your own food and about investigating waste.

- See Chapter 7 for home-school links concerning the topic of sugar, for ideas about investigations of electricity and traffic lights, and for visiting the supermarket to explore both science and ICT.

- In Chapter 9 we explored the idea of children going out of the classroom to look at materials in the school grounds.

## Some general ideas about going out of school

### What to take with you?

You will probably need to carry items to help the children to study the environment and to record what they find. Paper and pencils are often useful, but alternatives could be small notebooks with hard covers, or backing boards that allow children to write without a table or desk. Laptop computers or notebook computers are another alternative. Do you need to record specialist data, such as temperatures or light intensity? Digital equipment is safer and more robust than glass thermometers. If you intend to capture minibeasts or collect plant or other material, you need to think about suitable containers and maybe pooters for tiny creatures like ants. It is always worth listing the things you take out, so you can check they are brought back again.

### Who to take out with you?

An experienced class teacher can probably manage a class alone outside for short periods, but a student or newly qualified teacher will need extra adults. Who is available in your situation? Are there responsible adults like learning assistants, other student teachers, parents or carers? Are there adults available to support you at the place you are going to, such as education staff at a field centre? You always need to check with the school or local authority regulations about numbers of responsible adults accompanying parties of children. Some places you visit will also have rules about the number of adults needed for groups of children.

### How long to go for?

This depends on how far you are going, but a general rule is do short regular visits to a learning site, rather than long infrequent ones. Going to a natural site several times is better than going just once, since you can see the changes that occur with different seasons. The longer the visit, the more planning and preparation may be needed, for example, taking into account water and food, toilets and behaviour.

### How to get there?

Public transport needs to be booked in advance for some visits, especially if you want to travel by trains rather than buses. Do the children have special needs that need to be considered, such as mobility if they are very young, or wheelchair access and ramps/lifts? Walking to local sites can present problems if there are busy roads to cross. Hiring coaches can be useful but expensive. Is there a minibus that can be borrowed or hired, perhaps from a community group? Can you get a licence to drive it or borrow a licenced driver?

## Bringing the outside world into school

Although learning out of school is the main idea in this chapter, it should also be poss ible to bring the out-of-school setting into the school, by inviting outsiders to visit you in the classroom. Some schools invite in medical experts, others link with theatre companies, others still contact charities and health promotion organisations; some schools have potential for support from parents and governors; others make links with commercial companies.

## 11.1 Public places to visit – museums, galleries, interactive centres, science learning centres

### Where to go?

What are good places to visit for science and ICT opportunities? Museums and galleries are obvious places to start as they often have educational departments attached to them, to help busy teachers get the most from a visit. Visits to galleries may sound more about art than science, but there are often opportunities to cross the curriculum and provide science experiences alongside the artistic ones. Besides the larger national museums, like the British Museum or the Science Museum, there are many smaller ones that provide fascinating opportunities for teaching and learning. Football clubs often run visit schemes to support their communities and engage children's interests in sport and health matters. Leisure centres too may be potentially useful as contexts for both science and ICT, as most modern centres provide computer equipment for recording pulse rates and other data. History-based museums are often useful as resources for science, especially if they offer 'hands-on' sessions to school parties, so that children can touch and handle artifacts and explore materials practically. Zoos and aquaria often have education departments which may offer guided visits and spaces for classes to study, as well as study materials and worksheets. Theatres, music venues and opera houses may provide learning opportunities especially in terms of materials science as well as about sound. The buildings themselves offer the chance to explore both building materials and forces.

### One-off or regular visits?

It is also good practice to plan to visit some places more regularly, so that the trip is not seen as a special treat but more as part of the overall learning experience of children. Although this would depend on cost and distance, it is worthwhile establishing a link between real visits to places outside the classroom and virtual visits through the Internet and with the use of e-mail to maintain some communication. Quite often, it is useful to visit places seasonally, especially outdoor areas, as the light and the temperature may affect our ability to use the places in different ways. It is worth remembering that out-of-school visits can give teachers ideas about good practice in their own classrooms. Some interactive displays you encounter out of school, perhaps in a design museum, may give you ideas for similar displays within school. A role-play exhibit in a science centre may give you an idea for introducing role play as a teaching and learning strategy within your own lesson plans. It is important that you contact your local education authority for relevant and recent local advice.

## Designing monsters – a short case study

The Redcar and Cleveland City Learning Centre collaborated with local primary and secondary schools to design an activity to help bridge the primary-secondary transition (Brennan 2003: 10–12). Year 6 children in primary schools were involved in a number of school-based activities, such as creative writing, designing monsters and creating monster games. Then they were taken to the centre for half a day to undertake 30-minute activities, some involving ICT. A monster quiz was delivered to them, using PowerPoint. They were given Internet access to www.switcheroozoo.com, to let them make monsters from animal parts. They used Microsoft Publisher to 'mix heads, bodies and feet to create their own hybrid monsters. Skills included copy, paste, group/ ungroup, rotate and resizing' (Brennan 2003: 11). In the following year, children were introduced to Adobe Photoshop and this enabled them to make monster versions of celebrities (although how much science was involved in this is debatable).

## Information from the Internet – Field Studies Centres

Organisations that can help you with outdoor activities include the FSC (Field Study Council – see their website http://www.field-studies-council.org/ for further information):

Bringing Life into the National Curriculum
The FSC is a pioneering educational charity which welcomes over 50,000 children every year to its national network of Field Centres. Through its Centres, the FSC provides exciting oppor- tunities to explore at first-hand the world around us. Being out and about gives children an experience that can never be achieved through books, pictures or even television. Through fieldtrips, children feed their natural curiosity and develop their creativity. The world around them is brought alive. It becomes real, active and purposeful, has dimension and scale, and becomes the world to which they belong.

## 11.2  Buildings as starting points

### Shops

A good place to start is with children's own ideas. What do children know about what goes on in shops? Are they aware of science aspects of certain shops, such as the storage of things in shops? You would probably start with food shops, since the science here is fairly obvious – some food goes off easily unless it is kept in certain conditions. This can lead to investigations of cold storage, ideas about temperature and how to measure it (using ICT tools).

But what about the shops that sell clothing? Is there any science opportunity here, perhaps about materials and their properties? A brainstorming session conducted with

**TABLE 11.3** Brainstorming shops

| |
|---|
| What materials are shops made from, and why and where do they use: glass, wood, metal, concrete, plastic, fabric and any other type of material? |
| What layout does a shoe shop use that is specifically fitted to the activities of the shop assistants and the customers? |
| How are shops kept cool in summer and warm in winter? How are temperatures controlled? |
| How are shops lit up? What sorts of lights do they use? How are these different or similar to lights in school or in homes? Can you measure the light intensity in different parts of shops and relate this to purposes of these places? |

the children should provide some ideas for questions to ask the shop worker during the visit and then lead towards investigations when you get back to school.

Try adapting the brainstorm with children about the potential of food shops for studying science. See Chapter 7 for ideas about visiting a supermarket, but also think about the variety of types of food shops that are available in your own neighbourhood. The foods could be sorted into different groups and categories, ideally through using the children's own sorting criteria. This could lead to more scientific categories, if you thought it appropriate, but could also lead to the uses of ICT for sorting, such as branching keys like Softease Branch (www.softease.co.uk). Recent versions of this software come with lists of words, including a word list of foods, or you could start with pictures instead, if the children were younger and not yet able to read.

## Hospital schools – a student teacher placement

Any place where children have experiences can be a potential learning opportunity, although not all of them would be able to provide whole classes with visiting rights. A student teacher carried out a placement for a week at a hospital school in London, as an alternative to a placement in a normal primary school (there are at least three London hospitals that occasionally provide placements for student teachers in their education departments). Not only did she learn about the special provision needed for children in long-stay wards, but was also enthused by the care and attention given to children in these special circumstances, so that she might in future years apply for a teaching job in a similar context. Hospitals that have extensive children's wards also have the duty to provide learning opportunities for children who are forced to spend extensive time within these wards. Hospital schools often provide marvellous teaching and learning environments with access to scientific, medical and information-rich expertise. The special requirements of such schools are to do not just with the special learning needs of the children, but also concerned with the amount of differentiation needed, the need for plenty of work in very small groups or in one-to-one situations, and for flexibility in the opportunities planned for. Many hospital schools provide an ICT-rich environment so that children are given the opportunity to communicate more easily with the world outside the hospital.

## Garden centres

A visit to a garden centre could give children experience of materials and plants and their growing needs. Looking at the variety of pond designs and materials for building ponds in gardens should allow the children to think of the types of materials and their properties. Collecting data about these could be the start of a home-made database about materials in everyday life. The variety of plants for sale in a garden centre would be another starting point for creating a database. What sort of criteria would be useful as fields in a database on plants? The children could start with some of the categories on the plant labels, and then use their imaginations, creativity and curiosity to sort out some other questions to ask on a subsequent visit, or through writing letters or emails or phoning the garden centre.

## Parents as teachers

One of the most important places where children learn is in their homes. The home is often featured in educational texts as a place where children can be supported in their reading, especially at primary level, but increasingly children use computers in their homes for a variety of purposes. The home is also an important context for learning in science, since the hard and soft materials that make up our homes can be a starting point for the study of physical and chemical properties of materials, as well as the functions of these materials in modern societies. Some parents and carers will be able to support their children's learning in more specialist ways, through their own specific interests or jobs. It is possible for teachers to make use of some of this specialist knowledge and interest within the classroom – why not ask a bricklayer parent to come into the school during an open evening to support the learning you have been doing on bricks as hard materials or on forces and structures? Could a parent with an interest in weaving or dressmaking support the class in studying ways in which materials are joined together and how these materials respond to water? Can you make use of expertise in cooking, especially when it focuses on differences and similarities in preparing foods in several different cultures?

## Database creation from the home

Besides the branching key type of database, Softease provides another that uses records and fields. There are three different ways to use these databases: use an existing one, or use and adapt an existing one, or create one of your own. The Homes database has the following fields:

Type of house, e.g. cottage, detached, mobile home etc.

Garden, yes or no

Garage, yes or no

Age

Building material, e.g. brick, wood etc.

Chimneys

Windows

Communication, e.g broadband, cable, satellite etc.

Some of these fields are blank; others have examples of data within them, so that children can enter some data without needing to type, just through clicking with the mouse. This makes database creation much easier, as the data is entered accurately. Extra fields can also be added or existing fields deleted, so making the database easily adapted to the specific needs of the class or activity being planned.

## 11.3 The built environment

### Bridges

There are only about four main types of bridge structure: slabs, arches, cantilever and suspension. Model-making activities in the classroom can link science and design/technology, with some geography and history too. A visit to a bridge in the local environment can encourage children to explore not only the type of bridge, but also its history, reason for existence and material used in its construction. A problem-solving activity about bridge-making can encourage a creative approach among children. Start with thinking about the strongest way of making a roadway – or the simplest type of slab bridge. Conflicting ideas occur here, such as the weight of the material itself compared to the amount of weight it can carry. Paper models are useful in exploring the difference between lots of single sheets of paper, compared to different ways of folding paper to make it stronger. A spreadsheet would be a useful ICT tool to help record and graph the strength of different amounts of paper or card, then make predictions about the relationship between the amount of paper and the strength.

### Canals

If you are fortunate enough to be in a school near to a canal, there are plenty of opportunities for science and other subjects to be gained. There are, of course, dangers too: the water is deep; there may be dangerous machinery linked to the canal and lock gates; some parts of canals are lonely places where strange people may linger. However, the advantages are many. Historical aspects can be linked to science, through the various types of technology linked to the canal system, including bridges, locks, remains of horse-drawn barges, other boats. Nature too can be explored, through a study of the fish and animals living in the water, or the plants and bird and insect life along the banks.

## Roads and traffic

Geography and science can be linked through looking at traffic – movement and forces are the obvious traffic aspects, but think too about ideas from Chapter 5 on sustainability and the ways in which we can classify energy sources used by different types of vehicle. Traffic lights are an example of a link between science and ICT – electricity and control technology. The sounds made by traffic could also be investigated using digital sound meters – children could explore the relationship between, for example, different vehicles and the sounds they made, or the apparent speeds of vehicles and their sounds. Would it be possible with older children to approach ideas about gases in the environment and the connection between traffic near a school and air pollution, perhaps linked to the number of children suffering from asthma?

## Paths and playgrounds

Paths are a source of science about materials and their properties – this can be linked with the types of surfaces children experience in playgrounds – what kinds of surfaces are slippery, rough or smooth? What surfaces are better for different purposes? Cycle tracks can often present interesting design ideas that can link with the uses of ICT. Try asking children to design paths and cycle tracks to provide routes round busy road junctions. Use other design ICT (*My World 2 Garden* or *My World 3 City* programs, for example) to help them plan and record their own ideas about roads and paths, playgrounds and gardens. A visit to a playground can also be the starting point for learning about forces.

## 11.4  The natural environment

One of the responses of some city children to the natural environment is that it is dirty and boring. While studying plants and animals from books can lack excitement, children are easily stimulated by an active approach to natural places and things.

Visiting less organised open spaces will allow children to explore and investigate, to dig and make a mess, and to find out things for themselves. But you also need to plan

**TABLE 11.4**  Misconceptions about soil

| |
| --- |
| **Common misconception** Soil is just dirt. |
| **Usual age for misconception** 2–8 years. |
| **The scientific explanation** Soil is a complex mixture of organic and inorganic materials that can support a range of living things. |
| **Ways to address the misconception** Collect or buy a selection of different soil types and encourage children to observe them visually, with digital microscopes and with touch, to look at differences and similarities. |

visits carefully so that children make the best use of limited time and so that they are safe while in potentially dangerous surroundings. Make sure you find out about local rules and regulations on organising visits, both from the school and the place you are visiting.

## Adopt-a-tree

This is a useful technique to support learning through the environment. Find a tree in the local environment and revisit it over a period of time. Adopt it in the sense of getting to know as much about it as you can, from a variety of sources and aspects. Draw it (or take digital camera photos of it) in spring when the buds are growing and the blossoms start to appear, as a silhouette in winter when all that you can see is the shape of the branches, in summer when it is in full leaf and in the autumn when the leaves are turning brown. What animals and birds use it as a home during the different seasons? What can you find out about its history or the parts of the natural or built environment near it? What effects have these had on the growth of the tree or what effect has the tree had on its environmental neighbours? How can you measure different aspects of the tree, for example, the circumference of its trunk at different heights? What other ICT tools besides digital cameras can support the measuring and recording of the life of the tree? A digital light meter, for example, helps children to measure the amount of light received by plants on the ground beneath the tree.

## What's in the school grounds?

In some schools, the immediate environment can be a rich context for teaching and learning science with ICT. It is worthwhile starting with an audit of the grounds, to itemise what is there and what potential exists. I once asked a group of student teachers to carry out a simple audit, in the context of Education for Sustainability while carrying out a teaching practice. Try out something similar on your current school.

## Ponds and light

If there is a pond available in the locality or, even better, within the school grounds, then it can be studied using ordinary measuring tools and ICT digital devices in a number of ways. The most important starting point, though, is to ensure that the children themselves raise some of the questions that they then try to answer. Discussion is important to set the scene for studying outdoor areas. One example might be about the light that falls onto the pond and the effect of this light on the growth of plants. Children will usually know that plants need light to grow, but they could measure the amount of light and see whether the number of plants growing, or the sizes of these plants, seems to be linked to the intensity of light.

## Ponds and pH

Another example might be logging pH in a pond. Although an adult might have some idea that pH of the water (a measure of its acidity or alkalinity) could have an influence on the kinds of plants and animals living in it, children would need to be introduced to this idea of pH. What ideas would they already have of this concept? Some of the children might be familiar with the concept of pH from shampoos and cosmetics which are sometimes labelled with pH. It should be relatively simple to lead a discussion round from the pH that suits our own skin and hair, to pH levels in which other living things would also thrive.

## Nature trails

What about nature gardens and special scientific interest sites? There are many parks and open spaces that provide some opportunities for a study of plants and animals, especially birds, although there are also restrictions on the activities that children would be allowed to carry out. Try doing a search in your own local environment for natural sites that would be suitable for taking children to see and do. Are there nature trails already operating in some of the outdoor areas? What organisations exist to support children in studying in these natural areas?

## Creating an outdoor site

How about creating outdoor areas in the school grounds, with spaces for different classes in the school to make their own decisions about what to plant? Would you prefer to plant 'pretty flowers' or food crops, or large flowers like sunflowers, or to have a wild flower area that would attract birds and insects, or deliberate flowers that attract butterflies in the summer? Would an outdoor site planted with trees and grass be better for some schools, to provide shade and a relaxing atmosphere?

## Summary

In this chapter, you have seen why learning out of school is a good way to teach science and use ICT; how to organise visits to different types of places; how to use the Internet to support teaching and learning about places outside the school; and how other ICT tools can support the scientific study of materials and forces out of the school.

You should now be able to:

- Identify a number of suitable places out of the classroom to take children and the kinds of activities in them that will lead to learning in science and ICT.
- Plan lessons that encourage learning about forces and materials in the built and more natural environment.
- Use ICT tools to help children collect, organise and search data about materials in their environment.
- Co-operate with outside agencies in planning visits to support science and ICT learning.

## Web links

http://www.field-studies-council.org/

www.switcheroozoo.com

A fun site where children can switch the parts of animals around and explore how they would look and how they might function with different heads, legs and bodies.

www.softease.co.uk

A commercial site providing information about a range of useful educational software.

# 12

# Organising and managing science and ICT

## Introduction

This chapter attempts to draw together the various ideas, theories and lessons presented in earlier parts of the book and demonstrate the practical aspects of being a class teacher in a primary school. It summarises and organises the suggestions made throughout the book and tries to demonstrate how the chapters can be used to help you manage and organise the complexities of the classroom, so that you will be able to teach science and ICT effectively.

For example, we start by identifying big ideas in Chapter 1, such as the concept of 'energy'. We refer to the theory of social constructivism in Chapter 2, encouraging children to observe in different ways and then discuss their ideas. This leads to planning science lessons and using ICT in Chapter 8, where transformations of energy are investigated through the context of germinating seeds and the growth of a plant – energy from heat and light, plus energy from chemicals is transformed into further energy inside a plant, which can then be further transformed by an animal that eats the plant.

These suggestions require specific approaches to organising groups of children and to presenting the 'work' that they are required to do as well as the type of assessments you will want to make – such approaches and assessment techniques are described in this chapter.

## Learning objectives

By the end of this chapter you should be able to:

- Use strategies for managing practical work and discussion in science and ICT.
- Recognise the links between science and other curriculum areas.
- Construct schemes of work and draw up lesson plans.
- Assess children's progress creatively.

## 12.1 Managing the children

### Practical scenarios

Have a look at the following scenarios of things to do with a group of children. Each one raises a number of questions to encourage you to find creative answers that fit your teaching style and the learning styles most effective for your class or groups of children.

1   Bring in some seeds or feathers and ask the children to help you drop them and observe what happens. 'Is the same thing happening to all the feathers or seeds?' is one of the basic questions you need to help them ask. Looking at the similarities and differences in the way things fall will help children to answer this question. Helping them to express their observations using precise language will also help them make sense of what they see.

See Chapter 4 on flight for some follow-up ideas to this scenario, but try to suggest some other scientific and ICT scenarios that could be used as follow-ups. As well as what is happening, children need to be encouraged to investigate why things seem to be happening and raise further questions. Would you do this with a whole class? Would a small group in a space away from the classroom be better? How could children try dropping things from a greater height without endangering themselves? This starting scenario is about active observation, linked with children doing things and thinking/discussing the outcomes and then doing things again slightly differently.

2   Collect some balls (a variety of sizes and types) and let the children have one between two, asking one of them to drop the ball and the other to measure an aspect of its behaviour, such as the number of bounces before it stops, or the height of the first bounce. Encourage them to be precise about what to measure and to predict before measuring. Then put two pairs of children together and help them identify key questions they can investigate further; for example, do the bigger balls bounce higher than the smaller ones?

You need to set up the pairs so that they can then link up with another pair and compare their results. This helps them to consider alternatives to their own thinking and reduce the problem of one child feeling isolated from the discussion, since we ensure that each child has a chance to say something during this process. You may need to give the children precise times in which to speak and to listen, if they are at an early stage in the development of communication skills. Do the children manage to construct fair tests? Do they think the tests they carry out are fair?

3   Bring in three interesting, but not hard to draw, objects and place them in exact positions on a central table (for example, a cup, a teapot and a model cow). Give the children a short time to draw a sketch of the objects from one of six chairs around the table. Then move each child to the opposite place around the table and ask them

to sketch the objects again. Compare their drawings with each other in pairs and then into larger groups. Discuss the left/right placing and why things appear differently when you look from different places.

Children at an early age are usually egocentric – they only see things from their own perspective and think others see things in the same way. Looking at alternative ideas is an important part of scientific learning and physical looking can be a useful introduction to looking at more complex levels. In this scenario, children are not actively investigating, but they are observing and responding through drawings and then by discussing. Would it be possible to connect the appearance of the moon during its different phases to the reasons why objects appear different when viewed from opposite sides?

4    Find some snails or worms or woodlice in your garden or a patch of waste ground. Ask the children to watch them closely and see if they can describe how the animals move. Help them to raise questions, like:

How many legs do they have?

How do they move their heads?

What do you think they like to eat?

Make sure that children are aware of the need for sensitivity towards all living things before you introduce these minibeasts to the classroom. What previous experience have these children had of interacting with small animals or even with plants? It might be a good idea to introduce living things to small groups of children at first, to see what reactions they produce. This scenario should lead to children planning investigations to find the answers to some of the questions they have raised. How would you have prepared the resources to support the kinds of investigations they think of? See Chapter 5, section 5.2 for further ideas about investigating the behaviour of minibeasts.

| Directed Activity 12.1 Management issues | | |
|---|---|---|
| What are the alternative ways in which you could group children? For example, in pairs or threes, individually, in groups of six, as a whole class? | Scenario 1 | |
| | Scenario 2 | |
| | Scenario 3 | |
| | Scenario 4 | |
| What ICT tools would be useful? For example, a computer between two children, a digital camera, data-logging equipment for light, temperature, sound, a database program, a word processor, laptops, a computer suite? | Scenario 1 | |
| | Scenario 2 | |
| | Scenario 3 | |
| | Scenario 4 | |
| How much time do you think the activities would take? For example, half an hour only, two lessons of 20 minutes each? | Scenario 1 | |
| | Scenario 2 | |
| | Scenario 3 | |
| | Scenario 4 | |

## Managing questioning

One way of organising the learning encounters in the classroom is to employ a range of questioning strategies. Contexts for questions can arise in one-to-one assessment, or whole-class brainstorming of ideas, or group questioning that supports children in devising investigations to answer a particular problem. You can identify a series of question types, a set of strategies to encourage children to ask questions, as well as a set of ways to manage children's responses to questions.

## Attention-focusing questions

These can be factual ones that ask children to look at particular aspects of behaviour or features of objects or living things. They might also ask children to think, rather than just look, for example, when looking at a collection of shells:

'What did you notice that's different about them?'

When children observe in science, we are usually asking them to observe for a specific reason, not just haphazardly. We want them to notice certain things and a good way of helping them to do so is to focus on differences and similarities. This can be set up as a friendly competition, for example, listing the similarities and seeing who can find the most. Although this works well with inanimate objects, such as collections of materials, it can also be used in the flight context, for example, in comparing the appearance and flight patterns of birds. These could also be classified as 'comparison questions' (Feasey 1998).

## Open and closed questions

Open and closed questions are both useful at different times and for different reasons. Closed questions usually have one correct answer, or a yes or no response, for example, 'How many legs do insects have?' (the answer is six), but there are occasions when this categorisation is inadequate, as stick insects in classrooms often lose one or two of their legs, so it is possible to see five-legged insects. Another question that seems closed but in fact is not is, 'How long is it?' if the object in question is an earthworm.

Open questions often ask for children's ideas or alternatives that can be further discussed or investigated.

'What do you think?' is often a good way to start a question, followed by words like

'What do you think will happen if …?' or

'What do you think this will do if we …?' or

'What do you think makes this work?'

Some of these types of questions could be classified as action questions, since they may lead to children taking action, by exploring or investigating, in order to find better answers. It is sometimes useful to put together a series of questions to help children to set up investigations (see, for example, the teachers' guides to the SPACE project books SPACE 1995a,b,c):

'How do you think the clockwork toy works?'

Possible answer: A battery makes it go.

'How do you start it moving again?'

# Alternative answers in ICT

'How can we make it happen …?' is another good starting point, leading to some interesting alternative ideas of making things happen. This is also a useful question in ICT, since there are often a number of ways of carrying out certain activities. Even a search can be done in a number of different ways, which may easily give rise to different alternative answers. This business of alternative answers is important in many areas of learning, although it is also important to realise that there often is a correct answer to a problem and that the consideration of alternatives can help you to find this answer. But problem-solving activities should be provided so that children can learn this attitude themselves, rather than through the experiences of others.

# Children's responses to questions

Children's answers to questions could be oral, and lead to discussions, or they could be in other forms, such as through diagrams or drawings. Concept maps and concept cartoons are beginning to be used more frequently by teachers as ways to encourage children to respond. Logbooks and diaries, using both written and drawn examples, are also useful ways to help children respond to questions, for example, 'What does the moon look like?' Children could observe the moon on a series of different days or nights, sometimes at school, sometimes at home – they might draw it, or write about it, or collect pictures from magazines or the Internet and make a logbook of their various responses. Annotated drawings could also be used, for example, to help children answer the question, 'What happens to the sun during the day?'

# Discussions

Questioning often leads on to organising discussions – this can be a tricky thing to manage unless you plan for it. One of the problems in teaching children primary science concepts is how to help children explain an instance of an investigation disproving one of their predictions. If we fail to do this, it is likely that the new idea or explanation will be forgotten or discarded. Setting up discussion groups for science can be a useful way of getting children to think about alternative explanations. The subjects of these discussions can be taken from historical or current contexts. Children can be encouraged to search for some answers to their questions by using search facilities or selected websites. The questions raised and some of the answers presented should raise further questions in the minds of the children as well as allowing some to take up different sides in a debate and then try to present their own argument. ICT skills and resources could support the presentation, while electronic mail could support children in 'ask the expert' activities.

# Think, pair and share

An interesting idea used in some structured curriculum materials is that of 'Thinking, pairing and sharing'. The class is organised into pairs of children who are encouraged to talk to each other for set periods of time in order to sort out what they think is the answer to a set question or idea. One of the pair may then be chosen by the teacher in the sharing part of this activity. The teacher acknowledges the ideas of the children by writing them up on an interactive whiteboard or similar display screen and in some cases may ask children to agree or disagree with the statement, perhaps by using signals. The interactive whiteboard would be useful in allowing the teacher to move the answers around and link them together into categories. The children could signify agreement by giving a thumbs up sign and disagreement with a thumbs down. This device helps children to listen more carefully to each other as well as to instructions from the teacher. Giving each pair of children a small whiteboard and a single marker pen can further support this activity. During the pairing part, they write down their answer to the problem set and then, when sharing, they display their response to the rest of the class. This quiz aspect of this activity often helps to motivate the less interested children or those with a shorter concentration span. A teacher supported by a learning support assistant could use this session for some rapid assessment of some of the children and compare notes on significant progress after the lesson. The use of classroom support assistants during whole-class activities like pairing and sharing can be useful. It is sometimes the case that extra adults are wasted in whole-class sessions, only interacting with children during the group work periods and otherwise just passively listening to the teacher.

## Routines

Establish routines that you and the children can agree on. This decreases the time you need to spend explaining things and ways of working. It can also defuse confrontations between you and some of the children, especially if the children have agreed on standards of behaviour. Then a child who disobeys the rules is not just challenging the authority of the teacher, but is also going against the rest of the class.

## Gaining attention

Explore a number of ways of gaining the attention of the whole class – a clap, or series of claps getting softer, finger waving or clicking, a loud 'A-a-and …' or similar non-threatening word. There are many different signs and signals – one teacher of a rowdy class of six-year-olds used an antique silver bell that gave a quiet but recognisable sound which cut through any amount of noise and yet made you feel happy to listen to it. Another teacher of a Year 4 class used a 'rainmaker' instrument. This is a bamboo tube that contains tiny beads, which when it is inverted makes a sound like rain on a windowpane – a gentle sound, yet noticeable enough to attract the attention of the children in a positive way. She usually asked a child to operate the rainmaker too. Once you have the attention of the class, make sure you say your instructions clearly and simply. Can you collect other creative examples of attention-gaining tactics?

## Using resources

Do not lay out all your resources at the start of the lesson, but keep some in reserve. As soon as you put resources or equipment out on the tables, children (and students) will want to touch them and play with them; hence they can be a distraction if you are focusing on something else. Work out a good way of distributing the equipment just at the time you are going to need it. Establish routines for giving out and for collecting things back again.

## Thinking time

Allow the children some time to think before they try to answer questions; in fact, ensure that they do. Some children will put their hands up to answer before you have asked the question. This is an obvious sign of attention seeking, not thinking, so vary the ways in which you expect children to respond. (See Primary National Strategies 2003a and 2003b on speaking and listening.)

## 12.2 Crossing the curriculum to enhance children's learning

### Why cross-curricular links?

In May 2003, the UK Government produced a document called the Primary National Strategy (http://www.standards.dfes.gov.uk/primary/) in which six core principles for teaching and learning were introduced. One of these was, 'Develop learning skills and personal qualities across the curriculum, inside and outside the classroom' (http://www.standards.dfes.gov.uk/seu/coreprinciples2/). One reason for planning cross-curriculum links is that you can acknowledge the different 'subjects' in the curriculum as just a number of different ways of exploring and interpreting the world in which we live. So instead of looking at evaporation and condensation in science, or the weather patterns in geography, or how meteorologists use ICT to predict and communicate weather to us, we could examine our relationship with the weather from a variety of viewpoints and with a variety of critical and analytical tools. Another reason is that in primary schools, we are teaching younger children, rather than older ones with more abstract thinking skills. What these younger children need in order to learn effectively are interest, motivation and enthusiasm.

### Speaking and listening

A good classroom strategy is to set up a discussion group, with alternative ideas, preferably generated by a brainstorm from the class (but have some ideas to seed into the discussion if children do not seem to have thought about the problem; they may need some practical stimulus to get them thinking).The Primary National Strategy suggests introducing 'Talk Partners' as a speaking classroom technique (see the example of 'Think, pair and share' in Chapter 3). Why?

To enable children to participate in speaking – put children into pairs and allocate time for each to talk to the other at specific points in a teaching sequence, e.g. to share experiences, generate ideas, reflect on what they have just learned: retain pairs for a period of time, e.g. up to half a term, so that they establish routines, gain confidence and develop more extended turns.

(Primary National Strategy 2003a)

Key teaching points from the speaking strategy are:

Give the children time to think before they respond to questions.

Follow up children's contributions with further questions rather than repetition or ritual praise.

## Reviewing a cross-curricular website

Many websites involve a variety of subjects, or information and ideas that teachers could use for science, as well as in other subject areas. Choose a website to review using the list in Directed Activity 12.2. Add some categories of your own. Try to carry out the review using a school computer so you can identify the potential problems associated with speed and access at the school.

| Directed Activity 12.2    Reviewing a website | |
|---|---|
| Address of website | |
| Author of materials or group providing them | |
| Access requirements or issues about extra programs need to support the site | |
| Age range suggested or alternative age ranges considered appropriate | |
| Curriculum areas covered, including main area and subsidiary areas | |
| Accuracy of information, including depth of knowledge or variety of skills needed to be able to use the information | |
| Comments that you would make about any other feature of the site, for example, does it crash often, do the children find it very interesting etc. | |

## Measuring as a cross-curricular skill

Measuring is a skill that is needed in science investigations and has obvious links to parts of the maths curriculum. As a scientific skill, measuring needs to be closely linked with predictions and drawing conclusions. Measurements are carried out in science in order to answer a question and children need to think about the most appropriate ways of carrying out measurements. They may need to repeat measurements so that they can produce more valid data. They may need to use a range of measuring tools, depending on the scale that is required, for example, measuring weight (the force of gravity on an object) on a kitchen scales may be useful for some purposes, but for measuring other forces, they may need a more sensitive force meter (more commonly known as a spring balance). Some measurements can be made more accurately using ICT tools, such as digital thermometers or digital pulse meters.

## History and science

There are a number of ways in which science can link to history. 'Famous scientists' is one example that could link Internet searches with historical periods and with scientific discoveries. Materials and historical periods is another area for potential links, for example, thinking about and investigating the uses of different materials for holding water or other liquids by different people at different times. A study of containers used by the Romans, the Greeks or the Egyptians could lead to connections between history, science and design/technology (see Chapter 7).

| Directed Activity 12.3    Brainstorming other cross-curricular links | |
|---|---|
| Try to find useful links with art, such as drawings of flowers, using water colours or oil-based paints, in the style of artists like Monet, linked with the science of flowering plants and the parts of flowers. | Other art links: |
| Design/technology (DT) and science can be linked through problem-solving ideas, like designing and making a model bridge that can take a weight of 50 grams. Try finding starting points in a playground for DT and forces. | What other DT links? |
| Geography and science can be linked through big ideas like sustainability. Habitats like a river, the seashore and the canopy of a rainforest are other ways to connect the learning. The places where people live and the clothes they wear to keep warm or cool can be both scientific and geographical. | Where else do geography and science link up? |
| | *(Continued)* |

## Directed Activity 12.3   Continued

| | |
|---|---|
| Physical education (PE) has potential for linking with science, through the exploration of how our bones support our own bodies and how muscles help us to move. Health issues are also linked with science and the importance of taking exercise. | What would be the practical implications of doing scientific investigations during a PE lesson? |
| Religious education can be a starting point for science learning – think about the important significance of light in a number of religions, such as the Hannukah candle in Judaism, the Easter candle in Christianity, the Diwali puja in Hinduism. The ways in which different religions explain the origins of the world could be linked with scientific explanations and ideas about diversity of living things and evolutionary theory. | What other senses can be linked to religious ideas, e.g. are there specific foods you can identify that have religious significance? |
| Music has some obvious links with the study of sound and hearing in science. Try collecting musical instruments and exploring with the children how the sounds are made, how loudness is controlled, how pitch can be changed. | What instruments can you identify from non-Western traditions of music? |
| Try starting from a material like gold and see how many different areas of the curriculum could be connected with its study. | |
| Try another starting point, like the concept of colour, and see where that could support a cross-curriculum topic for a specific age range in a primary school. Try a brainstorming activity with a group of children and ask them to identify the subjects they think would be involved. | |

## 12.3  Planning lessons and schemes of work

### Differentiation

One of the most important features of modern teaching is differentiation, which is 'a process of identifying the most effective strategies for each learner' (Hollins and Whitby 2001: 166). There are two main ways in which this can be done in primary schools: differentiation by outcome or differentiation by task. Differentiation by outcome means that you expect children to complete different amounts of the same sorts of tasks, with some specific help being provided to some groups, while differentiating by task means that you set different tasks for different pupils. Many teachers manage this by setting core activities, then providing extension activities for the children who complete the tasks that the others are given. Cook and Finlayson (1999) quote an interesting model of differentiation in their book on ICT and classroom teaching. They mention a spiral model of support, core and extension in which all children do some part of the core activity, but where low attainers are helped to achieve that level. High achievers are expected to start at the core level and then 'continue to expand their knowledge and skill base' (Cook and Finlayson 1999: 83).

## The more able child

If teachers plan to differentiate by task, then children who can record more quickly may be seen as higher ability, rather than those who understand more – yet these may not be the same children. Another problem with the approach of extension activities is that the 'more able' children always have more to do than the others and may become resentful of this 'extra work'. So a solution is to provide 'other tasks', rather than 'more tasks'. See further discussion on 'ability and intelligence' in Chapter 2, especially about the theory of multiple intelligences.

## The problem of words

One of the problems you have to face when deciding on differentiation is that of vocabulary – which words do you use to describe children's differences? There are always new expressions coming through the various official and less official groups, some seen as more politically correct in various climates. 'Higher attainers and lower attainers', 'more or less able', 'average' child – none of these seems to describe the complexity of children's differences. Children progress in different ways and through different routes, but a teacher must try to provide tasks and activities that suit the apparent needs of the class and the individual.

## Children with lower abilities

Children do have different abilities in all sorts of ways. Some can run faster, others can play musical instruments better, others can write neater, others can understand computer games more quickly. If we take the theory of multiple intelligences seriously, we would never think of the 'lower ability child' and would never have a 'lower ability group' in the class. Differentiation in teaching should be about helping all children to learn more easily, taking into account the variations of their current levels of ability in these different contexts. Many ICT programs provide both visual and aural information to support learning.

## Progression

There are generic ways of planning lessons in any 'big idea', which may depend on the situation (e.g. a one-off lesson, or a series involving plant growth or change in life cycle, or growing crystals, or evaporation etc.). Examples were given of these in earlier chapters, as well as what would be likely to come before and what would come after. The emphasis for good teaching should be on adapting whatever scheme or planning format to your own needs in a school, using QCA headings, school systems of planning, published schemes of work or lesson plans from the Internet. Progression can be expressed and interpreted in several different ways. It could mean the outcomes expected are arranged in the order of difficulty, or the order in which the scheme deals with them, or it could mean the ways in which children change their ideas and become closer to the scientific understanding and the limitations of the theory. De Boo (in Keogh *et al.* 2002: 9–12) labels it 'progression' in children's ideas, but Hollins and Whitby (2001) also show how it is possible to label progression without reference to children, but instead to an expected progression in scientific ideas. It is, of course, important for a teacher to know what expectations we should have of children's ideas in science at different ages, but we cannot expect each child to follow the same route in learning.

## 12.4  Assessing progress

One of the most important aspects of good teaching is the ability to assess children's progress – after all, you only know you have taught something well if you also know that the children have learnt something. Assessment should always be for a purpose. It is often labelled as 'formative' – to inform your future planning; or 'diagnostic' – to help you identify specific errors or misconceptions; or 'summative' – to enable you to record and report progress to someone else.

### Why should children write about science?

The reasons for asking children to write things down or draw things in science needs to be clear both to the teacher and to the children. It can be frustrating for both if children are expected to 'write about it' just because that is what they always do. There should always be a clear and obvious reason for recording. One important reason for this, in terms of the teacher's needs, is that children's ideas help a teacher to recognise the progress they are making. Records made by children also help the teacher to identify misconceptions and then to plan ways of addressing these in future lessons. Student teachers are especially under pressure in some school placements to ensure that children produce as much 'work' as they are capable of. So it is tempting to use simple worksheets that children can easily fill in, rather than those that make them think. It is worthwhile to make pupil resources that help children to record their ideas and understanding as easily as possible. ICT tools can be useful here in providing writing frames to support those who write slowly.

### Conflicts in children's records

There might be conflict between a teacher's need for records and a child's desire to produce written or drawn outcomes. Children will often wish to produce correct answers to questions, so that they can be proud of their efforts and show them to others,

**TABLE 12.2** Teaching strategies to help combat misconceptions

| |
|---|
| **1** Examine alternative ideas to your own and see if they have any advantages or disadvantages. Provide children with alternatives and with time to discuss and re-examine their ideas. |
| **2** Draw a concept map of your ideas and see if you can show the links between the various parts. Help children to connect their own ideas together and also to compare their concept maps with those of others. |
| **3** Turn part of one of your ideas into an investigation and see if your results agree with your predictions. Grouping children together to plan and carry out investigations is not only effective, but also makes good use of the limited time available for science in the primary classroom. |
| **4** Make the imperceptible perceptible, perhaps by making a model of part of the event you are trying to investigate. Another way to do this is to help children to look at secondary sources of information. Provide a range of books about scientific ideas and processes. Support their ICT searches with well-chosen websites. Choose interactive CD-ROMs to support their thirst for knowledge and their curiosity about events. |

including their peers and parents/carers. So it will be in the child's interest to produce records with no misconceptions, while it may be in the teacher's interest to have the opposite outcome. A solution to this is the idea of drafts.

## Misconceptions

We must expect children to express misconceptions about certain ideas in science, because they try to make sense of their experiences using whatever ideas they have picked up. The task of a teacher is to help children identify their misconceptions and then provide ways to help them deal with them. At the same time, the teacher's task must be to record the ideas of the children, in order to be able to chart the progress they are making. Throughout the other chapters in this book, you have seen examples of misconceptions gathered together into tables (see Tables 8.3, 10.3 and 10.5, for example).

Although some misconceptions are specific to certain areas of science and will need to be addressed in specific ways, there are some general principles that can guide a teacher and help provide strategies for dealing with them (see Table 12.2).

## Assessment techniques in science (and ICT)

Here is a set of 15 techniques that could help you to assess children's ideas and the progress they make. Each technique is explained and exemplified – some are useful for whole classes or for individual children, others may be better used with small groups or pairs of children. Some work better with older children, others with younger ones.

## 1. Children's diaries

These could contain notes and drawings collected over a period of several days or weeks. These would differ from the daily diary which some teachers might have encouraged children to keep, in that:

**1**  The observations in the diary would concern one particular scientific situation, not a range of activities and interests.

**2**  The diary would not necessarily be in the form of written prose, but might easily involve drawings and diagrams, with notes, labels or brief explanatory or predictive statements.

**3**  Children would not need to record things every day, but only as often as the particular situation required (e.g. bean growth might not give any changes worth recording while the seed was awaiting germination, but might need daily or twice-daily examination during periods of rapid change).

The diary could be used for observations of slow changes such as:

- growth of plants from seeds;
- evaporation of water from containers;
- the changes involved in the metamorphosis of frogspawn to tadpoles into frogs, or from eggs to caterpillars to pupa to adult butterfly;
- the changes in appearance of the moon over a month;
- the changes in direction and length of shadows caused by the sun.

ICT tools that could help children to maintain these diaries would include word processors, or simpler versions such as word banks; digital cameras to record visual events; spreadsheets to help record and manipulate longer lists of data; and data loggers to record, for example, light intensity over a period of time. Weight could be measured more accurately with digital scales, perhaps?

## 2. Drawings and paintings of events

Children at different stages of development produce responses to some types of activity in drawings, which can easily be analysed for conceptual understanding. In the example of an investigation of the movements of model vehicles on slopes, a teacher might provide a template diagram for some pupils who dislike drawing and just ask them to fill in the cars, or even colour in the cars to show their results. More help given to pupils reduces the amount of information available to teachers in some cases, but in others makes some information available for the first time.

This technique might also be used for investigations of:

**1**  bouncing balls on different surfaces

**2**  the flight of model aircraft

**3**   the behaviour of light reflecting from a mirror or another surface

**4**   habitats in which certain minibeasts are found

ICT applications here could include paint programs and the use of clip art interlinked with word processors. Of course, digital cameras integrated with photo editors might replace the drawing itself, but there is value in asking children to undertake close observation and drawing as a scientific rather than just an artistic activity.

## 3. Labelled drawings

Children can be encouraged to explain the pictures they have drawn by adding a few words and lines or arrows to them. Examples of this might include:

**1**   Conditions for plant growth, where children have drawn the sun without making it clear whether it is the heat or the light from the sun that is necessary.

**2**   The operation of cogs, levers or pulleys, to show the directions in which the parts move.

**3**   The relative movements of the sun, moon and earth which cause daily, monthly and seasonal changes.

Paint-type programs can help with this, as can many other modern programs. Even recent versions of word processors allow you to insert diagrams, text boxes, clip art, and a selection of lines and arrows.

## 4. Observing group work

Watching and listening to children working in groups on practical investigations can provide useful assessments. A simple checklist might be appropriate, or a teacher might be able to use a mental checklist when observing for a short time for specific concepts or process skills. Examples of situations where this technique might be used include:

**1**   Observations of children working on electrical circuits, which could provide information about their understandings of the number of connections needed, i.e. the concept of bipolarity.

**2**   Investigations into preferred conditions for minibeasts, e.g. woodlice in a 'choice chamber' – a container with sections that are dark or light, dry or damp, warm or cold.

**3**   Testing the performance of home-made parachute models, where a number of variables need to be considered, fair tests constructed and collaborations are necessary between three or four children.

**4**   Deciding on the fields for a database with which to store and process information collected during investigations.

Digital cameras and tape recorders could support teachers in observing group work.

## 5. Structured discussions

When children working as groups, classes or individuals have carried out an investigation, they could be encouraged to report their findings and methods to the rest of the class or to another group of pupils. The teacher will often need to structure such discussions in order to explore their ideas and assess their understanding. Examples of these discussions might include:

1   Investigations with coloured filters, where children have looked at coloured objects through the filters and are reporting on their observations. The discussion would need to be structured so that a teacher could find out whether the pupils understood the functions of the filter as a kind of selective gate, letting some light pass through but stopping other light.

2   Reporting back on activities concerning weather observations, where the teacher would want to discover whether the pupils were beginning to link together some of these observations, e.g. a particular cloud formation often associated with rain, or rainbows occurring when rain and sun are present and in the right relative positions.

3   Discussion about how sounds are produced by musical instruments.

Interactive whiteboards are valuable tools to help teachers record and save the results of structured discussions with groups or whole classes. Word processors linked to projectors could be a useful alternative.

## 6. Specific questions to children

These can be used to elucidate the meanings of words or statements which the children have been using, or particular points which remain unclear from some other type of assessment technique. Examples might include:

1   Investigations on floating and sinking – 'What do you mean by light?' – where children might mean light/dark or light/heavy or lighter than something else.

2   In the context of activities about ourselves, 'What is bigger?' where it could refer to longer, wider, heavier or greater volume.

3   'What would happen if …?' questions, to encourage children to use their existing ideas in order to predict, and hence expose their existing ideas to the teacher, e.g. 'What would happen if there were no telephones?'

## 7. Children's writing

Free writing after investigations or structured writing can be used to encourage the recording of their hypotheses, predictions and conclusions. A structure could be imposed by the teacher asking specific questions which have to be answered in writing.

This structure can support those children who find writing difficult by including the words needed for the answers in the form of the questions. Examples might include:

1  'Which type of parachute travels more slowly, one with a larger or a smaller area?'

2  In the context of investigations with snails, 'What do you think snails like to eat? … Why do you think this? … How can you test if you are right? … Do all the snails like the same foods? … How did you tell the snails apart? … What did you discover? … Was your first idea about their favourite foods right?'

The obvious use of ICT here is word processors, but writing frames and word banks are interesting extensions of these. Clicker programs have been suggested in previous chapters to support children with special educational needs in writing and recording their ideas.

## 8. Completing drawings and diagrams

In some cases it may be useful to provide children with uncompleted drawings and asking them to add details. This allows teachers to focus on particular concepts and ideas and avoid the problem of children being unable or unwilling to draw. Examples might include:

1  Providing a drawing of a girl, with a desk lamp and a book, then asking the child to complete the diagram to show how the girl can see the book. The drawing might show whether the child understands the need for light in order for vision to occur, as well as the type of vision model the child is working with – active or passive eye model.

2  Completing a drawing of a room in a house, to show where electricity is being used.

3  Drawing of plants or animals which need to have important features added, such as flowers or eyes.

Again, there are some common ICT programs available that do this easily, for example, *My World Body* or *My World Face*.

## 9. Tape-recording children's conversations

This is a time-consuming technique, which would be used rarely to supplement other methods and perhaps to take examples to moderation meetings. Technical problems, such as background sounds, poor quality microphones and so on, also make the tape-recording of children in classrooms difficult. Examples of its use might include:

1  Recording a group which is working in an area away from the teacher, in a bay or corridor.

2  For children who write or record very slowly, but who are able to talk and can tape their ideas or answers to diagrammatic or written questions.

**3**   In an outdoor environment, when written recording would be difficult, e.g. in the rain or high wind.

## 10.  Problem-solving tasks

Evaluating the finished solution to a problem could be an example of assessment. In many cases, it would be skills that would determine the success of the task, but group co-operation, communication, perseverance and concentration would also be elements. Examples might include:

**1**   A bridge-making exercise where the model of the bridge could be assessed according to pre-specified criteria such as size of span weight to be carried, type of materials allowed, weight of materials.

**2**   A model wheeled vehicle, using various techniques for making the wheels run smoothly.

**3**   Making a choice chamber for minibeast investigations.

**4**   Making a hide for outdoor observations of birds and other animals.

Digital cameras make this simpler, as the photo of the completed model can be recorded and reproduced as often as you like.

## 11.  Interviews about instances

Talking to individual children about pictures or other stimulus, in situations where it may be difficult or unsafe to carry out practical activities, has often been used by researchers to discover children's conceptual understandings. Examples might include:

**1**   observations of the night sky and the phases of the moon

**2**   observations of the sun

**3**   road safety situations

**4**   dangerous electrical situations

The presentation of the instance is one way in which ICT can be used to support this technique. Many CD-ROMs and Internet sites exist that provide instances that could be used as starting points for questions to help assess progress in learning.

## 12.  Observation of non-verbal skills

Some children may be unable to express their ideas in English and yet are capable of understanding some science concepts. It is often possible to assess these science ideas by communicating with the child through gesture and demonstration, as well as by pictorial and symbolic methods. Pupils with less developed English language skills can still be encouraged to report on their activities, by showing what they have done, and can tentatively be assessed. Examples might include:

1    Investigations into electrical conductors and insulators – Venn diagrams could be used to sort materials on a yes/no basis.

2    In floating and sinking activities, a record could be made of the properties of the materials by putting them in different places.

3    Observations of animal movements could be demonstrated in gesture as an alternative to spoken language.

4    Demonstrations of measurements of simple differences between individuals could be done, along with a record of the numbers and sizes.

## 13. Concept mapping

Children can be taught to express their understanding of certain connections in science by making concept maps. These can be created by selecting a range of words about one area of science, then asking the children to connect these words together with lines which indicate the relationship between the words or ideas. Concept maps can be made with pictures instead of words. *Inspiration* is one piece of software specifically designed to support the production of concept maps.

## 14. Creating cartoons

A cartoon, made from a set of drawings and labels, can demonstrate a child's knowledge and understanding of phenomena like magnetism, as well as some skills concerning the sequencing of events in an investigation.

ICT programs like *Flash* are again specifically designed to help children create cartoons with animation, although PowerPoint is a more common program that can be used to set up sequences of events, demonstrating children's understanding of ideas.

## 15. Using timelines

Concepts like those of day and night can be assessed using timelines, where children are asked to show on a line some sequence of events. A timeline for a month could show children's understanding of the phases of the moon. A longer timeline could show children's ideas about the stages in growth and development of living things – the life cycle of a butterfly or the stages in development of a flowering food plant like a runner bean. *My World Cycles* software provides a very simple form of ICT tool for younger children to sequence their ideas about the development of some living things.

## Summary

In this chapter, you have looked at management strategies for science, exploring some scenarios for practical science activities; identified some reasons for supporting science learning through cross-curricular links; reviewed ideas about planning lessons and schemes of work; been introduced to reasons and techniques for assessing pupils and recording their progress.

You should now be able to:

- Manage scientific practical learning activities in a number of different settings.
- Recognise the potential for cross-curricular teaching and learning and understand how these links can enhance meaningful learning.
- Plan lessons and schemes of work for science, using simple frameworks and pupil resources.
- Understand a number of techniques that can be used to assess children's progress in science learning, using ICT tools in some cases.

## Web links

http://www.standards.dfes.gov.uk/primary/
The National Primary Strategy.

http://www.standards.dfes.gov.uk/seu/coreprinciples2/
Core principles in the National Primary Strategy.

www.standards.dfes.gov.uk/schemes
QCA site for schemes of work in the National Curriculum.

# Appendix: Qualifying to teach in the Foundation Stage, Key Stage 1 and Key Stage 2

## 1. Professional values and practice

### Standards statement

1.1 They have high expectations of all pupils; respect their social, cultural, linguistic, religious and ethnic backgrounds; and are committed to raising their educational achievement.

1.2 They treat pupils consistently, with respect and consideration, and are concerned for their development as learners.

1.3 They demonstrate and promote the positive values, attitudes and behaviour that they expect from their pupils.

1.4 They can communicate sensitively and effectively with parents and carers, recognising their roles in pupils' learning, and their rights, responsibilities and interests in this.

1.5 They can contribute to, and share responsibility in, the corporate life of schools.

1.6 *They understand the contribution that support staff and other professionals make to teaching and learning.*

1.7 They are able to improve their own teaching by evaluating it, learning from the effective practice of others and from evidence. They are motivated and able to take increasing responsibility for their own professional development.

## 2. Knowledge and understanding

### Standards statement

2.1 They have a secure knowledge and understanding of the subjects they are trained to teach. For Key Stage 1 and/or 2, they know and understand the curriculum for each of the National Curriculum core subjects, and the frameworks, methods and expectations set out on the National Literacy and Numeracy Strategies. They have sufficient understanding of a range of work across the following subjects: history/geography, physical education, ICT, art and design/design and technology, performing arts and Religious Education to be able to teach them in the age range for which they are trained, with advice from an experienced colleague where necessary.

2.2 They know and understand the Values, Aims and Purposes and the General Teaching Requirements set out in the National Curriculum Handbook as relevant to the age range for which they are trained to teach. They are familiar with the Programme of Study for Citizenship and the National Curriculum Framework for PSHE.

2.3 They are aware of expectations, typical curricula and teaching arrangements in the Key Stages or phases before and after the ones they are trained to teach.

2.4 They understand how pupils' learning can be affected by their physical, intellectual, linguistic, social, cultural and emotional development.

2.5 They know how to use ICT effectively, both to teach their subject and to support their wider professional role.

2.6 *They understand their responsibilities under the SEN Code of Practice, and know how to seek advice from specialists on less common types of special educational needs.*

2.7 They know a range of strategies to promote good behaviour and establish a purposeful learning environment.

2.8 They have passed the Qualified Teacher Status skills tests in numeracy, literacy and ICT.

## 3.1 Planning, expectations and targets

### Standards statement

3.1.1 They set challenging teaching and learning objectives which are relevant to all pupils in their classes. They base these on their knowledge of: the pupils, evidence of their past and current achievement, the expected standards for pupils of the relevant age range and the range and content of work relevant to pupils in that age range.

3.1.2 They use these teaching and learning objectives to plan lessons, and sequences of lessons, showing how they will assess pupils' learning. They take account of and support pupils' varying needs so that girls and boys from all ethnic groups, can make good progress.

3.1.3 They select and prepare resources, and plan for their safe and effective organisation, taking account of pupils' interests and their language and cultural backgrounds, with the help of support staff where appropriate.

3.1.4 They take part in, and contribute to, teaching teams, as appropriate to the school. Where applicable, they plan for the deployment of additional adults who support pupils' learning.

3.1.5 As relevant to the age range they are trained to teach, they are able to plan opportunities for pupils to learn in out-of-school contexts, such as school visits, museums, theatres, field-work and other employment-based settings, with the help of other staff where appropriate.

## 3.2 Monitoring and assessment

### Standards statement

3.2.1 They make appropriate use of a range of monitoring and assessment strategies to evaluate pupils' progress towards planned learning objectives, and use this information to improve their own planning and teaching.

3.2.2 They monitor and assess as they teach, giving immediate and constructive feedback to support pupils as they learn. They involve pupils in reflecting on, evaluating and improving their own practice.

3.2.3 They are able to assess pupils' progress accurately using, as relevant, the Early Learning Goals, National Curriculum level descriptions, criteria from national qualifications, the requirements of Awarding Bodies, National Curriculum and Foundation Stage assessment frameworks or objectives from the national strategies. They may have guidance from an experienced teacher where appropriate.

3.2.4 They identify and support more-able pupils, those who are working below age-related expectations, those who are failing to achieve their potential in learning, and those who experience behavioural, emotional and social difficulties. They may have guidance from an experienced teacher where appropriate.

3.2.5 With the help of an experienced teacher, they can identify the levels of attainment of pupils learning English as an additional language. They begin to analyse the language demands and learning activities in order to provide cognitive challenge as well as language support.

3.2.6   They record pupils' progress and achievements systematically to provide evidence of the range of their work, progress and attainment over time. They use this to help pupils review their own progress and to inform planning.

3.2.7   They are able to use records as a basis for reporting on pupils' attainment and progress orally and in writing, concisely, informatively and accurately for parents, carers, other professionals and pupils.

## 3.3 Teaching and class management

### Standards statement

3.3.1   They have high expectations of pupils and build successful relationships, centred on teaching and learning. They establish a purposeful learning environment where diversity is valued and where pupils feel secure and confident.

3.3.2   They can teach the required or expected knowledge, understanding and skills relevant to the curriculum for pupils in the age range for which they are trained.

3.3.3   They teach clearly-structured lessons or sequences of work which interest and motivate pupils and which: make learning objectives clear to pupils; employ interactive teaching methods and collaborative group work; promote active and independent learning that enables pupils to think for themselves, and to plan and manage their own learning.

3.3.4   They differentiate their teaching to meet the needs of pupils, including the more able and those with special educational needs. They may have guidance from an experienced teacher where appropriate.

3.3.5   They are able to support those who are learning English as an additional language, with the help of an experienced teacher where appropriate.

3.3.6   They take account of the varying interests, experiences and achievements of boys and girls, and pupils from different cultural and ethnic groups, to help pupils make good progress.

3.3.7   They organise and manage teaching and learning time effectively.

3.3.8   They organise and manage the physical teaching space, tools, materials, texts and other resources safely and effectively with the help of support staff where appropriate.

3.3.9   They set high expectations for pupils' behaviour and establish a clear framework for classroom discipline to anticipate and manage pupils' behaviour constructively, and promote self-control and independence.

3.3.10  They use ICT effectively in their teaching.

3.3.11   They can take responsibility for teaching a class or classes over a sustained and substantial period of time. They are able to teach across the age and ability range for which they are trained.

3.3.12   They can provide homework or other out-of-class work which consolidates and extends work carried out in the class and encourages pupils to learn independently.

3.3.13   They work collaboratively with specialist teachers and other colleagues and, with the help of an experienced teacher as appropriate, manage the work of teaching assistants or other adults to enhance pupils' learning.

3.3.14   They recognise and respond effectively to equal opportunities issues as they arise in the classroom (including challenging stereotyped views, bullying or harassment) following relevant policies and procedures.

# References and further reading

Ager, R. (1998) *Information and Communications Technology in Primary Schools*. London: David Fulton Publishers.

Ager, R. (2000) *The Art of Information and Communications Technology for Teachers*. London: David Fulton Publishers.

Ainley, J. (1996) *Enriching Primary Mathematics with IT*. London: Hodder and Stoughton.

Anderson, M. (2002) *A–Z of Key Concepts in Primary Science*. Exeter: Learning Matters.

Bennett, R. (1997) *Teaching IT at Key Stage One*. Oxford: Nash Pollock.

Brennan, A. (2003) 'A Monster Transfer Project', *Primary Science Review*, 380, 10–12.

Byrne, J. and Sharp, J. (2002) *Using ICT in Primary Science Teaching*. Exeter: Learning Matters.

Cook, D. and Finlayson, H. (1999) *Interactive Children, Communicative Teaching: ICT and Classroom Teaching*. Bucks: Open University Press.

Crompton, R. (ed.) (1989) *Computers in the Primary Curriculum*. London: Falmer Press.

Crook, C. (1994) *Computers and the Collaborative Experience of Learning*. London: Routledge.

Davies, J. (1995) 'Does SATing damage children's self-esteem? A four-year cross-sectional study', *Education*, 3(13), June 51–5.

DfEE (1997) *Connecting the Learning Society*. London: HMSO.

DfEE (1999) *The National Curriculum Handbook for Primary Teachers in England: Key Stages 1 and 2*. London: QCA.

DfEE/QCA(1999) *Information and Communication Technology; The National Curriculum for England*. London: HMSO.

DfEE (2000) *Science Teacher's Guide Update*. London: QCA.

DfES (2002) *Framework for Teaching Science Years 7, 8 and 9*. DfES Crown Copyright.

DfES (2003) *Excellence and Enjoyment: A strategy for primary schools*. DfES Crown Copyright.

Donaldson, M. (1984) *Children's Minds*. London: Fontana.

Duncan, S. and Bell, A. (2002) *The little book of experiments*. London: Hodder and Stoughton.

Ellis, J. (1989) *Equal Opportunities and Computers in the Primary Classroom*. London: Equal Opportunities Commission.

Feasey, R. (1998), in Sherrington, R. (1998).

Feasey, R. and Gallear, B. (2001) *Primary Science and Information Communication Technology*. Herts: Association for Science Education.

Fox, B. (2003) *Successful ICT Leadership in Primary Schools*. Exeter: Learning Matters.

Frost, R. (2002) *IT in Primary Science*. Hatfield: Association of Science Education.

Glover, D. and Miller, D. (2001) 'Running with Technology: the pedagogic impact of the large-scale introduction of interactive whiteboards in one secondary school', *Journal of Information Technology for Teacher Education*, 10(3), 257–76.

Goodison, T. (2002) 'Learning with ICT at primary level: pupils' perceptions', *Journal of Computer Assisted Learning*, 18, 282–95.

Griffen, D., Inman, S. and Meadows, J. (2002) *Teaching for a Sustainable Future*. CCCI London South Bank University.

Hafford, A. and Meadows, J. (1999) 'Electronic mail provides positive role models', *Primary Science Review*, 57.

Harlen, W. (2000) *The Teaching of Science in Primary Schools* (3rd edition). London: David Fulton Publishers.

Harlen, W. *et al*. (1977) *Match and Mismatch: Raising questions*. Edinburgh: Oliver & Boyd.

Harrison, M. (1998) *Co-ordinating Information and Communications Technology Across the Primary School: A book for the Primary IT Co-ordinator*. London: Falmer Press.

Hartley, K. (2000) *Senses in Living Things*. Heinemann First Library, Oxford: Reed Publishing.

Hollins, M. and Whitby, V. (2001) *Progression in Primary Science*. London: David Fulton.

Howe, C. (1995) 'Learning about physics through peer interaction', in Murphy, P., Sellinger, M., Bourne, J. and Briggs, M. (eds) *Subject Learning in the Primary Curriculum*. London: Routledge.

Jensen, B. and Schnack, K. (eds) (1994) *Action and Action Competences as Key Concepts in Critical Pedagogy*. Copenhagen: Royal Danish School of Educational Studies.

Johnsey, R., Peacock, L., Sharp, J. and Wright, D. (2002) *Primary Science: Knowledge and understanding*. Exeter: Learning Matters.

Keogh, B., Naylor, S., De Boo, M. and Barnes, J. (2002) *PGCE Professional Workbook: Primary Science*. Exeter: Learning Matters.

Leask, M. and Meadows, J. (eds) (2000) *Teaching and Learning with ICT in the Primary School*. London: Routledge.

Littledyke, M., Ross, K. and Lakin, L. (2000) *Science Knowledge and the Environment: A guide for students and teachers in primary education*. London: David Fulton Publishers.

Lodge, J. (ed.) (1994) *Computer Data Handling in the Primary School*. London: David Fulton Publishers.

Maxwell-Hyslop, M. (2003) *Fish Go Woof*. London: Hodder.

McBroom, P. (2003) Using an Interactive Whiteboard for Topic Work at Key Stage 1 Mirandanet web resource www.mirandanet.ac.uk

Moseley, D., Higgins, S., Newton, L., Tymms, P. (*et al.*) (1999) *Ways Forward with ICT: Effective pedagogy using information and communications technology for literacy and numeracy in primary schools*. University of Newcastle.

Murphy, C. and Beggs, J. (2003) 'Children's perceptions of school science', *School Science Review*, 84(308), 109–16.

Murphy, P. (1999) *Primary Science Review*, 60, 2–3.

Nash, G., Wilson, A. and McDougall, R. (1997) *The Internet Guidebook*. London: Peridot Press.

NCET (1994a) *Portable Computers in Action*. Coventry: NCET.

NCET (1994b) *Highways for Learning*. Coventry: NCET.

NCET (1995) *CD-ROM in Primary Schools Initiative: Titles Review*. Coventry: NCET.

Nuffield Primary Science (1995) *Living Things in Their Environment: SPACE Teacher's Guide (ages 5–7 and 7–12)*. London: Collins Educational.

Osborne, J., Black, P., Meadows, J. and Smith, M. (1993) 'Young children's ideas about light and their development', *International Journal of Science Education*, 15(1), 83–93.

Osborne, J., Smith, M., Black, P. and Meadows, J. (1994) *SPACE Research Report – the Earth in Space*. Liverpool: Liverpool University Press.

Osborne, J., Wadsworth, Black, P. and Meadows, J. (1994) *Primary SPACE Research Report on Children's Ideas about the Earth in Space*. Liverpool: Liverpool University Press.

Ovens, P. (1987) 'Ice Balloons', *Primary Science Review*, 3, 5–6.

Papert, S. (1980) *Mindstorms: Children, computers and powerful ideas*. London: Harvester Wheatsheaf.

Peacock, G.A. (1998) *Science for Primary Teachers: An audit and self-study guide*. London: Letts.

Peacock, G.A. (1999) *Teaching Science in Primary Schools: A handbook of lesson plans, knowledge and teaching methods*. London: Letts.

Plant, M. and Firth, R. (1995) *Teaching Through Controversial Issues*. Nottingham: Nottingham Trent University/British Agrochemicals Association.

Preston, C. (1995) *21st Century A to Z Literacy Handbook*. London: Institute of Education.

Primary National Strategy (a) (2003a) *Speaking – Making it work in the classroom*. DfES/QCA Crown Copyright.

Primary National Strategy (b) (2003b) *Listening – Making it work in the classroom*. DfES/QCA Crown Copyright.

Pollard, A. (1997) 'The Basics and an Eagerness to Learn: A new curriculum for primary schooling', SCAA International Conference, London, June 1997.

QCA/DfEE (1998) *Information Technology: A scheme of work*. London: QCA.

QCA (1998) *Planning and Organising Science*. London: QCA.

QCA/DfEE (2000) *Curriculum Guidance for the Foundation Stage*. London: QCA/DfEE.

QCA (2003) *Information and Communication Technology Teacher's Guide*. London: QCA/DfEE.

Ratcliffe, M. and Lock, R. (1998) 'Opinions and Values in Learning Science', in

Sharp, J. and Byrne J. (2001) *Primary Science Audit and Test*. Exeter: Learning Matters.

Sharp, J., Potter, J., Allen, J. and Loveless, A. (2002) *Primary ICT: Knowledge, understanding and Practice*. Exeter: Learning Matters.

Sharratt, N. (1994) *Ketchup on Your Cornflakes*. London: Scholastic Children's Books.

Sherrington, R. (ed.) *ASE Guide to Primary Science*. Cheltenham: Stanley Thornes.

Sherrington, R. (1993) *Primary Science Teachers' Handbook*. London: Simon & Schuster.

Sherrington, R. (1998) *ASE Guide to Primary Science*. Cheltenham: Stanley Thornes.

Shuard, H. (1985) *The Homerton Logo Manual*. Cambridge: CUP.

Skinner, B. F. (1950) 'Are theories of learning necessary?' *Psychological Review*, 57, 193–216.

Somekh, B. and Davis, N. (eds) (1997) *Using Information Technology Effectively in Teaching and Learning*. London: Routledge.

SPACE (1995a) *Electricity and Magnetism Teachers' Guide*. London: Nuffield Primary Science, Collins.

SPACE (1995b) *The Earth in Space Teachers' Guide*. London: Nuffield Primary Science, Collins.

SPACE (1995c) *Life Processes Teacher's Guide*. London: Nuffield Primary Science, Collins.

Straker, A. (1997) *Children Using Computers (2nd* edition). Oxford: Blackwell.

Taylor, R. P. (1980) *The Computer in the School: Tutor, Tool, Tutee*. New York: Teachers College Press.

Trend, R., Davis, N. and Loveless, A. (1999) *QTS: Information and Communications Technology*. London: Letts.

Twining, P. (1999) 'ICT: another misguided initiative?' *Primary Science Review*, 60, 30–32.

Underwood, J. (ed.) (1994) *Computer-Based Learning: Potential into practice*. London: David Fulton Publishers.

Underwood, J. and Brown, J. (eds) (1997) *Integrated Learning Systems: Potential into practice*. London: Heinemann.

Vygotsky, L. S. (1986) *Thought and Language*. Cambridge, MA: MIT Press.

Watkins, C. (2003) *Learning: A sense-maker's guide*. London: Association of Teachers and Lecturers.

Watkins, C., Carnell, E., Lodge, C., Wagner, P. and Whalley, C. (2000) *Resources for Supporting Effective Learning*. London: Routledge.

Wenham, M. (1995) *Understanding Primary Science: Ideas, Concepts and Explanations*. London: Paul Chapman.

Wood, D. (1998) *How Children Think and Learn* (2nd edition). Oxford: Blackwell Publishing.

Woodford, G. (2000) 'Enriching food and farming with ICT', *Primary Science Review*, 62, March/April.

# Abbreviations

**BECTa** British Educational, Communication and Technology agency

**CLA** Classroom learning assistant

**CT** Class teacher

**DfEE** Department for Education and Employment

**DfES** Department for Education and Skills

**FC** Foundation Curriculum

**GTC** General Teaching Council

**NC** National Curriculum

**NGfL** National Grid for Learning

**QCA** Qualifications and Curriculum Authority

**QTS** Qualified Teacher Status

**QTT** Qualified to Teach

**TTA** Teacher Training Agency

**SENCO** Special Educational Needs Co-ordinator

**VTC** Virtual Teachers Centre

# Science glossary

**Acceleration** – the change in velocity (or speed in one direction) of an object. In other words, when things go faster or slower, or travel in a circular motion, they are said to be accelerating or decelerating.

**Alive** – an organism, animal or plant, that carries out the seven life processes of movement, respiration, sensitivity, growth, reproduction, excretion and nutrition.

**Atoms** – all matter is made of tiny particles called atoms. Atoms contain smaller particles called protons, neutrons and electrons.

**Cells** – every living thing is made of cells, each of which is a kind of building block in which chemical reactions take place, allowing life to exist.

**Circuit** – the path along which an electric current flows.

**Concepts** – ideas we use to make sense of the world around us – they can be considered to be the way we understand events or phenomena.

**Digestion** – the process by which food is broken down by a digestive system. It happens through physical processes (teeth, for example) and chemical ones (saliva and gastric juices, for example).

**Electromagnetic spectrum** – visible light is one type of electromagnetic radiation; the others are gamma rays, X-rays, ultraviolet rays, infrared rays, microwaves and radio waves.

**Electromagnetism** – when an electric current flows in a wire, it creates a small magnetic field near to that wire. This electromagnetic effect is used in electric bells and motors, audio and video tapes, loudspeakers and computer disks.

**Energy** – the capacity for doing work. Energy can be described as being of various types, for example, chemical, kinetic, potential, heat, light, sound and nuclear. It is measured in joules.

**Gravity** – a force that attracts objects towards each other.

**Kinetic theory of matter** – briefly, this suggests that all matter is made of atoms and molecules and that these tiny particles move or vibrate. The hotter they are, the faster they move or vibrate.

**Light** – a form of electromagnetic radiation. It is needed to help us to see.

**Molecule** – a group of two or more atoms, chemically joined together, that make up a substance. A hydrogen molecule contains two atoms of hydrogen; a water molecule contains two hydrogen and one oxygen atom.

**Particles** – all matter is made up of small particles called atoms or molecules. These are too small to be seen, but they are thought to vibrate, or move around, depending on whether they are in the form of solids, liquids or gases.

**Process skills** – skills concerning investigating in science, including observation, testing, measuring, communicating and interpreting.

**Radiation** – heat can travel by radiation, conduction or convection – radiation is a form of energy transfer, for example, the way that light and heat travel from the sun to the earth.

**Ultraviolet** – a form of electromagnetic radiation.

**Wavelength** – the length of the wave between one high point and the next.

**Work** – children's work is a misnomer, since children are at school to learn, not to work. In science, work is done when a force moves; the amount of work is equal to the magnitude of the force multiplied by the distance moved.

# Index